Dyslexia-Escaping The Forest

A child's view lost in the trees

Rhona Macdonald

Published by Twalpennie Worth Limited, March, 2019
ISBN: 9780473469115

Copyright © 2019 by Rhona Macdonald
All rights reserved. No part of this publication may be reproduced, stored in or introduced into a retrieval system, or transmitted, in any form, or by any means (electronic, mechanical, photocopying, recording or otherwise) without the prior written permission of the publisher. This book is sold subject to the condition that it shall not, by way of trade or otherwise, be lent, resold, hired out, or otherwise circulated without the publisher's prior consent in any form of binding or cover other than that in which it is published and without a similar condition including this condition being imposed on the subsequent purchaser.

Editor: Danielle Anderson
Typeset: Greg Salisbury
Book Cover Design: Judith Mazari
Portrait Photographer: James Ensing-Trussell

DISCLAIMER: The thoughts and feeling portrayed within this book are genuine to the time and setting that they occurred. They are not fully aligned to the thoughts and feelings I experience now while reflecting on this period.
My father worked long hours to support and provide for his family, so my mother is the ever-present parent figure within these words. It may appear that I hold my mother accountable for a sizable proportion of my pain, and that may be legitimate for the young person whose voice speaks throughout this book. It is not warranted of the present time.
I have tried to be sincere to the thoughts, feelings and beliefs I experienced as I progressed through school – ones I no longer identify with – and as a result my mother does not come across as the wonderful person she truly is.

To Mrs Jane McDowell, my life saver.

1993: "Everyone in this classroom has the capability and experience to write a novel."

2018: This is mine Mrs McDowell, sorry it took so long. It took longer to write it than it did to live through it. Both challenges are now complete.

Testimonials

Rhona's book is a heartbreaking story of a child struggling with dyslexia in the '80s. But more than that, it's the story of a child, like most children in the '80s, who was almost never listened to or treated with respect by the adults in her life.

This book will show you what it feels like to have dyslexia, and it will also show you what it feels like to have the help in exams which are now routinely given (reader, writer and extra time).

Rhona's compelling story absorbed me from start to finish, and really showed me what Dyslexia was, and is, like for her.

—Liz Sedley, **Creator of *Dyslexia Gold***

Rhona's childhood journey gives the reader a fresh perspective on growing up with the challenge of dyslexia. Her clever, 'inner monologue' narrative tells her story in a child-centred way, as daily dramas, vivid imagination and relationship dynamics are shared, filtered through the different stages of growing up.

For educators, this is a timely reminder of the powerful role we have in the classroom and our responsibility to enable every single child in our care to thrive, no matter what their circumstances.

Her story highlights the power of understanding a learning disability and having the skills and willingness to personalise a programme to allow a young person to reach their potential. The more stories that are heard, the better understanding of dyslexia we will all have.

—Sarah Wakeford, **Humanities Teacher (20 years experience), New Zealand**

Contents

Dedication III
Testimonials IV

Preface 1

Part One - *The Worst Years* 5

Part Two - *The Bridge* 143

Part Three - *The Better Years* 161

Epilogue - *The Best Years* 261

Acknowledgements 269
Afterword 272
Author Biography 274
More About the Author 275

Preface

"Any man's life, told truly, is a novel..."
—**Ernest Hemingway,** *Death in the Afternoon*

In 2005 I started writing, a task that I'd never enjoyed for reasons that will become clear as you read these pages. I wrote for myself – to separate, acknowledge and accept my childhood years, the ones that I was told time and time again were "the best years of my life." I wrote in an attempt to cleanse the soul, to rid myself of the demons, to finally and definitively put to rest these painful and upsetting memories in a bid to be able to look forward with some confidence and a little self-pride. Essentially, I wanted to switch off the lights, turn down the music, and be comfortable with what remains true of my childhood.

I wondered if I had remembered things worse than they really were. My parents said that my numerous misprompted actions were just a form of attention-seeking; you will be the judge of which view is correct. Your conclusion, however, will no longer affect me – or so I will keep reminding myself.

I thought the task would be fulfilled within a long weekend or even a few weekends. I thought I'd pick it up, do some work, and then put it back in the closet for a period of a few months or years where it could return to its dormant state, out of sight and out of mind. I was, following my personal tradition, wrong! In truth it consumed me during dog walks, airplane flights, cycling, and swimming. It invaded films that were meant to be watched passively and music that was played to be heard. It ran uncontrolled during every second of relaxation time, even my sleep. It haunted me, tightening its death grip over and over again. I longed to be free of the task, either by completing it or by closing the file and pretending I'd never started. I tried both options. Writing or not writing quickly became an inescapable task.

Whenever the file was closed, memories oozed back to my mind and demanded attention. Even when I was busy at work, I'd be jolted back to a past feeling by an innocent remark made in jest which not so long ago would have shattered me. While it no longer wrecked me, it did unsteady me. I knew the comment was not truly meant – or was it? Their opinion should not matter, but yet somehow it did, at least to me. After all these years, it still made a mark. I still cared. I was still ashamed of who I am.

I've felt like a failure for most of my life, in most aspects of that life, and to give up on the whole task of revisiting and addressing my past would just add to the already-too-long list of failures. Oftentimes I wavered and stalled. Rationally, it seemed pointless to dredge up the memories that were smouldering just beneath my consciousness, but something kept me moving forwards. I was supported and encouraged to continue to write – to keep opening more and more suppressed memories – by dear friends, without whose support I would never have gotten this far. And so I kept writing.

If you are young and struggling, I hope these words will give you a little strength, a little encouragement to keep fighting,

Preface

keep plodding onwards, keep holding a little belief in yourself despite whatever the occupants of this harsh and cruel world are screaming at you daily, especially when surrendering or ending the pain seems so much more achievable.

To those who were present throughout this recount and may see themselves in the less-than-perfect characters presented, I invite you to reflect on your actions and the reactions they created. You will of course have your own perspective, which you may even call truths, but this is my truth. For those who see themselves in a thoughtful, caring character, thank you for the kindness you have shown me. I have not exaggerated any characters. The reader may equally dismiss any part within this retelling, but again, this is my story, my view, my one-sided opinion.

As I brush my hair every morning, I look in the mirror and tell myself that I am smart. I try to remember those who have shown kindness and helped me before those who have hurt me so very deeply. It could be claimed that writing these words is selfish; on some days, I would agree. But, do not be mistaken. We are all selfish; some of us just fail to recognise the trait.

"If the reader prefers, this book may be regarded as fiction. But there is always the chance that such a book of fiction may throw some light on what has been written as fact."
—**Ernest Hemingway,** *A Moveable Feast*

> # Part One
> *The Worst Years*

Rhona Macdonald

1

England, 1995

"Ladies and gentlemen, welcome aboard British Airways flight number fifteen to Hong Kong, continuing on to Sydney."

I listened to the announcement coming out over the intercom as I sat on my first Boeing 747. I was eighteen years old and despite everything I had faced, I had actually made it. I had survived. I was heading to Australia.

"If you haven't already done so, please stow your carry-on luggage underneath the seat in front of you or in an overhead bin. Please take your seat and fasten your seatbelt."

I was already in my window seat, my small bag under the seat in front of me. My seat belt was fastened over my empty bladder. I was ready. This was a moment I had waited for ever since I was eight years old, when I had pointed to Sydney on World Map Day and claimed that it was where I wanted to live. I watched my fellow passengers get themselves organised, many dragging out books to read. I would not be pulling a book out of my bag; I may never read a book again.

My mind drifted back to when I was very young and my family went to Britain's largest aviation museum near

Chapter 1

Cambridge. One of the many, many planes there was the supersonic Concorde, which could fly from London to New York in about three hours. It took us longer to drive to Edinburgh from our hometown. This plane would not be as fast – the flight would take twenty-six hours – but that didn't matter. All that mattered was that I was on it.

The 747 was moving now, with me in it. "Shortly, the crew will be demonstrating the safety procedures. It is important, and we ask for your attention…"

I paid attention. How rude, not to look at the person talking to you. No book could be so good, or so important, or so enjoyable that reading couldn't be paused for a few minutes to take notice of the emergency exits and life jackets.

My school years, as I had been told so many times that I'd long ago lost count, "were the best years of your life." Why, in my experience, was that not true? I sorely hoped they were the worst years of my life. But adults knew best, and what if they were correct? That thought was terrifying. What horrific events were ahead of me? How could it get worse?

The engines roared, and we sped down the runway. The nose of the plane lifted and the body and tail followed. My stomach remained on the tarmac at first, but it quickly caught up with the rest of me. I watched London get smaller and smaller, its roads like veins wriggling over and under themselves, and then it was clouds – grey clouds, then darker grey clouds – before we burst into the sunlight. Life as I had known it was lost below, trapped beneath the grey clouds bursting with their tears onto the energetic city.

I basked in the warmth of the blissful sunshine. It was so toasty. It melted my mask away, my "I do not care" mask that I'd worn for years. I did care. I always cared far too much; that was one of my many problems. But now I let my new mask, my smile, settle in its new home. I fought back the water that threatened to leak from my eyes and quietly whispered to myself:

"OK, here we go, the best years of your life start now – enjoy."

2

Scotland, 1988

Easter break was late in the season during the year of 1988, but the ski fields of the Cairngorms still boasted snow. The so-called local area was full of strange faces that flocked to the village of Grantown-on-Spey with their tales of far-away hometowns – towns that I'd never heard of and had no idea if they were from this land or another. Our town always seemed to be full of visitors, flaunting the fact that the place they called "home" was somewhere other than our sleepy little village.

Grantown, as it was locally known, was a tourist haunt that boasted being the first Georgian-planned village of the Scottish Highlands. It had been a holiday destination of Queen Victoria and was home to the famous Speyside salmon, which returned to their origins within the fastest flowing river in Scotland each year after swimming away to warmer climates during the winter. Their presence guaranteed the best freshwater salmon in Scotland, which in turn guaranteed a high price tag to fish in the river – although it did not guarantee the best fishing in Scotland. The visiting fishermen appeared to enjoy their excursions, or at the very least they enjoyed the hip flask of

Speyside malt that kept them warm while they stood in the icy waters, waiting for a bite.

To me, it made sense that our village was a tourist destination; it was idyllic-looking, with its old-fashioned Georgian buildings. The town of Grant was nestled between the mountains deep in the heart of the Scottish Highlands, remote and removed from the city of Aberdeen which lay eighty miles to the east and the town of Inverness thirty miles to the west.

Grantown had one of most of the things you would need. One castle and one museum. One war monument in the centre of its one square. One high street, which was home to its one tourist information office, one newspaper office, one chemist, and one post office. One GP surgery and one hospital/hospice. One police station, which was open from 9:00 a.m. to 5:00 p.m. One primary school and one grammar school. There were a few newsagents and a few supermarkets, which I would learn in time were actually just really large corner shops. There was a modest collection of churches but only two graveyards: the "old cemetery" and the "new cemetery." Someone had clearly underestimated how many people would die in Grantown, or more accurately how many would actually live in Grantown.

In an effort to live up to the touristic expectations, the one high street – helpfully named "High Street" – was littered with arts and crafts shops flogging the same knick-knacks and souvenirs you could find anywhere in Scotland. Grantown did have lots and lots of hotels, each boasting its own bar and many with restaurants. It had an even greater choice of pretty walks and endless breathtakingly scenic views. No doubt about it, Grantown was a holiday destination, but somehow I was not on holiday there. I merely called Grantown "home."

I grew up in an ordinary family. I was the youngest child of

Chapter 2

three and the only girl. My brothers Calum and Evan were six and four years older than me respectively. My father was a master coachbuilder and was born in the area, which he so loved, and my mother was from a farm sixty miles away; she moved into Grantown at the age of twenty-five after marrying my father, who was thirteen years her senior. Mum was a housewife – she cared for the kids and looked after the house, everyone always knowing their role and what was expected of them. Yet I always felt unsure as to what I was meant to be doing, where I fit in. Nobody ever showed me the list of dos and don'ts, so I followed the example set by my older brothers. It made sense to me that whatever they could do, I would be able to do. We were made from the same stuff after all, from Dad and Mum, and our parents assured us we could do anything we wanted if we tried hard enough. As a young child, I believed them unquestioningly.

My brothers both skied well naturally, and I was sure my own natural ability was only seconds away from making an appearance. My school teachers all preached the same thing: I needed to try harder and improve my concentration, which would enable me to keep up with the class and move on to new exciting tasks rather than repeating old boring ones and falling further behind. By giving extra concentration and effort while I skied, I reassured myself that I too could glide effortlessly down the steep slope and not be frightened of taking a wrong turn onto a run which would end up with me on my backside – or, even worse, perched on the back of my skis and completely out of control, facing directly downwards on one of the dreaded Black Runs of Doom.

I had a secret weapon this particular ski season as well: the technologically pioneered Atomics Arcs. I'd had my eye on them for a while and had impatiently waited for my brother to grow out of his, which took too long for my liking. They were impressive, and if I could not ski on these, I feared I would face doom and failure once again.

That Easter my brothers went skiing and therefore so did I, determined as ever not to get left behind or excluded from any potential fun. My brothers' plans did not include me, though, and at eleven years old I was not allowed to ski by myself. Instead, the Organisational Queen, as we called our mother, organised for me to go up the mountain with a girl from Primary Three – the year that left me behind – along with her parents and little brother.

I started the day determined to successfully ski down the mountain, but my new skis were very long and I struggled to keep upright. As the morning wore on, my skiing companions got faster and I got slower. I couldn't keep up, but I knew that I had to. The ski runs all looked the same to me, and although I knew the only way off the hill was down, there were some runs closed due to inadequate snow coverage – and, of course, there were the Black Runs of Doom that were best avoided altogether.

Soon, I lost heart. Why did I bother trying? It was all too hard. It was late in the season and the snow, like me, was tired; it had lost its fluffiness, its movement, its flexibility, its forgiveness. Worse, it had left traps of bare rocks and patches of ice as a warning to all that it was not safe to proceed beyond that point.

Finally it was the last run before lunch, and I was relieved. I wondered if I would be able to go home or if I'd have to ski for the afternoon as well. I couldn't remember the plan. I was tired and needed the toilet, but I just had to make it down one more run. We went off the White Lady and down the Chicken Run. As usual, my companions lead. Were they trying to leave me behind? Was I really that slow? Were they just trying to lose

Chapter 2

me? I regretted upgrading to these new skis – they seemed so long and so hard to turn. *Maybe next year,* I thought, *I might return to my shorter commits.*

Maybe next year, I'd develop my natural ability to ski.

I knew that I would have to keep skiing, though. I'd have to try again next year. My parents had invested too much in our skiing – the lifts up and down the mountain, the lessons, the ski passes, the news skis that were bought for one brother and then passed down the pecking order to justify the original price tag, the boots that were just mine as I never fit the hand-me-downs, and my brand new all-in-one ski suit that Santa had brought me that year. I would have thought Santa could have stashed a little of the natural ability I so dreamed of in the pockets, but it appeared he had forgotten to do so.

I just had to survive this last run, and then we would get lunch. I had started out confident, but then I usually did start confident, backed by supportive parents, stating their pride in us kids and willing us to reach for the stars.

I never made it to the bottom of the run.

3

When would I learn? Falls are harder when you start off confident. Maybe it's better not to set yourself up for fall after fall, failure after failure. If you don't expect to be any good, you won't be so disappointed when you fail and fall yet again.

I found myself lying next to the snow fencing that I had collided with, one ski escaping away from me down the hill. My legs felt distant to my hips; I hoped one or both would be hanging off, cut by the super strong wire that held the fencing together, the white snow stained red. Then they would feel sorry for racing off and leaving me behind. It was obvious they were better than me – they had clearly made that point on the first run of the day. Just like in school, they had repeated the lesson again and again, as if that was going to help me improve. Did they think I was slow because I wanted to be slow? Did they really think I was trying to be a problem by dragging behind? If my legs were gone, they would be sorry for their behaviour.

I rolled over to check whether my limbs were attached. To my disappointment, my legs were both still there. The toe which had dismissed its ski looked like it had twisted to face the wrong way, but that would just be me seeing things; I could imagine almost anything. I spent a lot of time at school doing

Chapter 3

this. My teachers called it "time-wasting" – me dreaming of a better life, a life where I did not fall as often. A life where I was good, where I could do simple stuff like the rest of my class like read or write or even talk. I never thought I was greedy, I didn't want to be better than them. I simply dreamed of being as good as them.

A passer-by stopped – a few stopped actually. One had my escaped ski and another was helping me sit up. I felt a little wobbly, but essentially fine. I was used to getting back on my feet and carrying on through life being a little unsteady.

I had had the same wobble after I'd completed my 3000-metre swim the previous year. It had taken me over an hour to swim the full distance. I could have done it much faster, but I had been warned not to set too fast a pace in case I ran out of energy. I also swam slowly to delay my return to the classroom. Nevertheless, once I completed the task and placed my feet on the bottom of the pool, reinstating my vertical position, I felt wobbly, a little unsteady, like I was on a boat riding the waves.

I had always been a good swimmer. Our powerful mother could not swim, and – determined we would not grow up with the fear of water that she harboured within her – she took us each to swim lessons before we started school. I was just over three years old by the time she could feel pleased, if not exactly happy. Pleased that her third child was able to swim, but not happy that I could swim out of her reach and out of her sight and into the responsibility of the lifeguard. "Like a duck to water," they said. I don't remember learning to swim. In my mind, I could always just swim; it was easy to me.

The swimming teacher informed me that the 3000-metre swim would be my last long-distance badge because these arduous swims took a long time to complete and caused me to miss regular class time, which was precisely why I wanted to keep swimming. But no, the teachers knew better, and what was better for me was that I continued to struggle and fail in regular class rather than doing something I could succeed in. To a ten-year-old, this seemed totally unfair. I was good at swimming; I was not good at school.

Apparently, I was not good at skiing either. My lifesaving Atomic Arcs had failed to turn me into the natural skier of my dreams.

For as long as I could remember, I had always struggled at school. I had always been behind the rest of the class, I found everything to take more effort than it appeared my peers had to dedicate to the task. Not only did I struggle and fail daily at school, but now it seemed I was failing at the weekends, at the activities that were meant to be fun. Skiing was supposed to be fun.

I was so very tired of falling and failing. Why was it always me? I wished I could give up everything. All I wanted was to go to sleep and never ever wake up.

4

The mother of the girl that I had come skiing with and spent the morning trying to catch up with appeared next to me. She looked just as tired as I was. I was tired of skiing and sick of life; her eyes told me she was just sick and tired of me.

With support from the few strangers who had stopped and remained as my audience, I was hoisted up to a standing position. I eased my toe into the front of the ski binding and thumbed my heel down to catch the back binding. My leg screamed, and the scream raced through my body and out of my mouth before I could catch it. I sat back down on the snow. I was urged to try again, and I got to my feet but failed to stand.

I fought back the tears as someone skied down to raise the alarm and summon help. The mother sent her own daughter down to meet the rest of the group and let them know what had happened; that she was stuck with me, that I had held everyone up all morning and now claimed I was unable to stand. I was pathetic.

I knew what was coming: a skier with a red sledge. I'd seen them many times, speeding down the slopes. I'd always wondered what it would be like to be a good enough skier to tow others, or even to be wrapped up in the red sleeping bag on the sledge. Today, part of my question would be answered.

The skier and the sledge took ages to arrive. "A lifetime long," according to my family's traditional phrase for waiting a longer-than-expected time. "Oh, don't go into the post office now, Mrs AB, the queue is a lifetime long."

Many people stopped and asked if they could help, but we assured each one in turn that help was on the way. My red sledge duly arrived and I was bundled up and strapped on tightly, a little too tightly over my full bladder. The journey was long. A lifetime long. *What a strange saying,* I thought. The front of the life queue is death, so as we travelled down the hill I thought of this lifetime long, about the peace that could be found after only an extra unexpected ten minutes' wait. In my mind, which longed to get to the front of the life queue, my journey down was a lifetime long for some lucky people.

Even if we had begun our journey at the very top of the hill, which we hadn't, it should not take this long to reach the bottom. My head bounced and smashed, dulling any pain in my leg; in fact, my leg did not concern me. I hoped and prayed it was broken so that I might be spared ever having to ski again, but I feared it was not painful enough to merit a break. After all, I was certain I had broken my wrist during a caravan trip when I was around five or six years old, but I had been wrong then too.

My family went on many caravan trips when I was young, although to be honest I don't have a clear memory of these happier times. I was the baby of the family and our caravan holidays were very much over by the time I was eleven. My brothers were then too old for caravanning, so I was just unlucky to have been born last, and that they remembered these holidays and I did not.

I do recall the ongoing fight for a window seat with my

Chapter 4

brothers, all of us claiming car sickness and therefore the requirement to sit by the window. The answer was always the same. We would sit in our seat for thirty minutes, then move so that everyone got their turn sitting by a window and, by default, a turn at sitting windowless in the middle. The car dashboard clock was the timer. The same problem always occurred. Once Evan was sat in the middle and the clock indicated time to move Evan would not budge, which I took to mean it must be the best seat. Therefore, Calum and I then wanted to be in the middle. Seating arrangements caused the biggest issue each and every holiday.

According to photos of me at different tourist spots, my caravanning holidays occurred from the ages of two to seven years old. One album shows a tour that took us from John O'Groats, the northernmost point of Scotland, to Land's End, the most southern piece of the mainland British Isles. Another set shows a hovercraft whose destination was the Isle of Wight. There are chocolate factories, zoos, eating two ice creams at once, and me wearing whatever I had failed to get into my mouth – just as well that I'm only wearing a nappy in that photo. I'd been to pick (and eat) strawberries, and the story often retold is that we made ourselves sick. Miniature villages, water parks, stony beaches, and wildlife shows also feature in a large number of pictures.

I have one clear recollection of sitting behind Mum in a window seat, watching boulders and trees fly by. I used to try to focus on one in front and then follow it as I passed. It was as I was turning back to watch a tree that I saw the wheel of the caravan fall off and bounce over the boulders and rocks. I cried out that we had lost a wheel. My parents said "oh, I don't think so," but I was sure, absolutely certain. So were they. They were the adults, so I was wrong. I pleaded that they should stop, and then they would see that I was right. They never stopped. I was silenced with a sweet and went back to trying to watch trees as they passed.

Hours later we got to the campsite, where father noticed the hubcap was missing from the caravan wheel on the passenger side.

On arrival at every caravan park, the caravan needed to be parked and set up before anyone got to explore. This routine always struck me as odd. Why go through the bother of ensuring the caravan was level and had power and water before investigating the site? What if the site was rubbish and we had to move? We would have wasted all that time setting up the caravan for nothing. I suggested we should look around first, but it didn't matter what I thought. My job was to watch the air bubble trapped within the liquid of the level and say when it was between the two little black lines.

On the fateful trip where I injured my wrist, there was a big wooden castle in the caravan park playground. I was out with my brothers, making friends with the other kids who were holidaying there. I got on okay with the kids in these caravan parks. They did not know I was daft. They never saw me cry over school work that I could not do. They never knew I couldn't read properly, spell properly, or at times even speak properly. They never knew that sometimes I found even breathing difficult and controlling my thoughts almost impossible. Instead, I was just the annoying little sister that was always tagging along with her brothers.

A game of tag developed and teams were organized. Most of the kids were bigger than me, so I knew I had to think of ways around the "rules." They were faster, but I could hide in smaller places so I was not tagged too often. Eventually I went to run across the drawbridge, and suddenly there was a kid at each

Chapter 4

end blocking my entrance and exit. I was going to be caught. I didn't want that, so I leapt off the side of the bridge with a mental vision of hitting the ground and running off. Cats could do this effortlessly; leap, land and run. I thought I'd see if maybe I could do the same – I'd never tried it before, so maybe I'd find I had some talent.

The bridge was quite high; it took a while for me to hit the ground. I wasn't a cat though. I remained where I landed, took a deep breath and started screaming.

Initially my brothers did not believe that I'd jumped from such a height, but I had two witnesses. Everyone was amazed; I was warmed by their amazement, and then shattered as they claimed I must be mad to think that jumping from such a height was a great idea, or even an okay one. I wanted to be brave or courageous, not stupid or mad. My arm hurt even more.

My brothers took me back to the caravan, where I changed my story and now claimed that I'd fallen off the drawbridge. No one would believe I was stupid enough to jump off because I hoped to develop cat-like powers before I landed, and I could not think of any other good reason to jump. My brother had not seen the fall/jump, so the story was mine to tell as I wanted. I could just call the other kids liars.

I knew my arm was broken; it was the sorest thing I'd ever done to myself. Mother asked me to move my hand, which I could, although it caused even more pain. But because I could move my hand, my mother – a woman with no medical knowledge other than watching *Casualty* – determined that my arm was not broken, and that no further attention was required. I was told to go to bed and stop complaining so I didn't ruin the holiday.

My leg didn't hurt as much now as my arm did then, so surely it could not be broken. And now I was being stretchered off the hill due what would certainly turn out to just be a bruise on my leg. I was wasting everyone's time. I would be ridiculed when this got back to school. In fact, there was probably enough material to make my entire not-yet-arrived summer a nightmare.

5

We finally made it to the bottom of the hill. On the count of three I was scooped up off the red sledge onto an ambulance stretcher, the doors were closed and then we were on the move.

It was very alienating, lying down with no windows to look out of. Two people sat to my side, one with her arm in a sling and the other tending to paperwork. I asked when I would be able to go to the toilet. Neither helped me, and neither answered me – both simply looked at me as if I'd just asked the impossible. I wondered what was wrong with that question? How come everything I asked was always so stupid? I did not expect to go to the toilet there and then, but I did need to go and wanted to know when such a thing might be possible. But no, as per usual, I got a look that said "you're mad" and my question went unanswered.

We stopped at Aviemore, the town at the bottom of the hill. Sling girl got out and my mother, of all people, popped her head in. A doctor asked me how I was; I explained that I needed to use the bathroom. He replied by jabbing my leg with a needle and explained that it would improve things. I did not ask how a needle in my thigh would relieve my bladder, but he was a doctor so he must know best. He unwrapped my leg, informed me that the next part would hurt, and released the clips on my boot one by one. I had four clips, and a shudder of pain echoed through me as each was released.

The doctor informed Mum that I would have to go to Inverness Hospital for an x-ray, who in turn informed me that she and Dad would come to Inverness as soon as possible. Her voice sounded concerned – she even looked concerned. Did I need to be concerned? I was concerned that I needed the bathroom, but no one else was concerned about that so maybe there were more concerning things to be concerned about. She left, the doors were closed, and I was on the move again with paperwork man.

The road trip to Inverness did not take as long as it would have in a car. I lay there trying to work out if we were speeding, with the blue lights flashing and the siren sounding, but deep down I knew they would not be on; I was not important enough for blue lights and sirens. I tried to stop my brain from overthinking, or even just thinking, but I was never able to control my mind – it controlled me. All my school report cards said that I needed to concentrate more, to have more focus, but I found controlling my mind impossible.

The ambulance jostled, and with it my bladder. I desperately tried to hold everything in. I didn't want to have an accident and dirty my new snow suit. Despite the fact that I had asked to go to the bathroom, despite the fact that no one would help me, if I dirtied my suit, it would be my fault.

It had been my fault in Primary One, when I was four and a half. I had needed to go to the bathroom. I didn't care what the time was, or whether or not I was time-wasting, I needed to go. I asked to go to the bathroom, and the teacher said no. I asked again, and again, and again, and again. Each request was met with another variation of no. The responses did not change

Chapter 5

the need. After breaking a sweat and many unanswered prayers for the clock to move faster towards 3:00 p.m., I went to the bathroom without really being aware that my body had taken control of my mind. My body was looking after itself as I was no longer able to look after it, much like a baby can't look after its own bodily needs.

I sat statue still on my chair, terrified, petrified something would fall out of the bottom of my winter trousers and onto the floor. I wished to be invisible. I wondered where poos went after they were flushed away; you never see them again. Maybe I could exit like that. Although I'd prefer to take off floating high like the balloon that so frequently escaped from my hand even when I was holding it extra super tight. How did that balloon always so easily escape and float far away from me?

Finally, after what felt like forever, the bell went. I held my statue pose. The teacher announced to the class that I could go to the toilet now; I did not announce that I'd already been. I very, very slowly picked up my bag and jacket and walked very, very slowly towards and through the classroom door, past the bathroom door and towards freedom, confirming to the teacher that I did not need to go to the bathroom and was in fact trying to waste time.

Faithful Mum was at the gate to meet me, and I told her what had happened. She wanted to go and talk to the teacher, but I had escaped from training class for the day and only wanted to go home and wash. I claimed that returning would just makes things worse. If the other kids were to find out what I had done, what I was made to do, then they would never play with me ever again. I reminded her I had to go to school for years with these kids.

We started to walk slowly towards the safety of home. Mum kept asking me why I did not ask to go to the bathroom, but she did not hear me say "I did ask to go." Then, the question changed to "why did you not just go?" I had two answers to that: "I did" and "She said no – that I was wasting time." Mum assured me that people would have known what I had done; they would have smelt it. I didn't think I could feel any worse until she said that. That was something I'd not thought of. I hated myself. We continued in silence, apart from my snots and snuffles as I tried to regain control of my disobedient self.

We arrived at the safety of home where I bathed and made Mum promise not to tell anyone – no teacher, no Dad, no brothers. I would pretend this had never happened. If the kids at school said anything, I'd call them liar, liar, pants on fire.

I assured myself I'd forget about this day. I had forgotten about lots of days in the past. I knew I was almost five years old, and I'd already forgotten more than half my life. Today would be the same. I worked out that I might have to wait until I was ten years old, but I would eventually forget about this horrible day of Primary One.

Sitting in that ambulance and trying to keep control of my bladder, I could still recall the shame and dirtiness of what Mother now referred to as "my accident" as if it happened yesterday. I was still trying to understand why it was *my* accident. Yes, it did happen to me, but an accident is something that happens without awareness or planning. That might explain my existence in this world and my current situation within it, but that day in Primary One I knew I needed to go and I asked, I pleaded, and the teacher said no. Why does that make it an accident? Why does that make it *my* accident, my fault?

No, I would not have another accident. But if the ambulance didn't hurry up, I may not have control over that either.

6

Once again, I found myself praying to a non-existent God who had never fulfilled any of my previous requests. The doors opened and another man in a white coat came to look at me and ask questions about the skiing accident.

"Did you hear a crack?" he enquired.

"Yes, I broke a bit of fence."

"And you stood afterwards?" he asked, looking at the paperwork he had been handed.

"Yes, almost twice."

"What happened the first time?" He looked at me.

"Somebody helped me up and I got my toe into position, but my heel hurt a lot when I tried to snap it into my ski binding."

"And the second time?"

"It was like my foot was not there at all, I fell down."

"We'll need to take a special kind of picture that looks at bones. It's called an x-ray. Is that okay?" he asked.

"Okay. I've never had an x-ray before."

"It doesn't hurt. It will show us the bone and then we can see if it's broken, okay?"

"Okay."

A nurse in a white dress was concerned that I was sweating

and said something about my blood pressure. She was talking to the kind doctor though, not to me.

"I desperately need to pee." It came out a little too urgently, a little too panicked. The nurse had not even been talking to me. How very rude of me to speak when not spoken to. Mum would be cross if she found out.

"I'm sorry," I continued to blurt out. "I needed to go to the bathroom before I fell. I've told everyone and no one can help." I tried to stay as calm and polite as possible, remembering my mother's training about social situations. My eyes were filling with the all-too-familiar fluid.

The nurse was back before I'd really finished my polite explanation. I hadn't noticed she had left.

"I'm afraid it will have to be a bedpan," she explained almost apologetically.

"I don't care, I just need to go," I replied, overwhelmingly grateful for her help with my current emergency.

"Do you want me to cut your ski suit, or would you like to try and get out of it?"

I was wearing the pink and purple all-in-one ski suit that I had gotten for Christmas. It was not a hand-me-down, it was mine – all mine, just mine. She had given me the choice to try and get it off or be cut out. My choice – all mine, just mine.

"I would like to try and not damage it." I had felt that Mum would be cross if I tore it skiing, or rather falling while trying to ski, so I thought I better not allow it be ruined. If the nurse had just cut it maybe that would have been okay, but I figured then I'd have likely gotten told off for not stopping her.

"Okay, let's see what we can do. Let me know if your leg is sore." She helped me wriggle out of the suit, offering support, encouragement, and congratulations with every limb I freed. It was surprisingly easy. When three of the four were liberated, she

Chapter 6

slipped a cool bedpan under me. I'm sure I only had seconds to spare. A cool, relaxing, relieving feeling instantly washed over me as my bladder emptied and my sweat cooled.

Time didn't matter anymore; I had all the time in the world to wait. Nobody needed me, and I needed no one. I lay waiting for whatever life would bring next.

I and my makeshift bed/trolley were moved along to the x-ray. "Smile," the non-white-coat-wearer said. I wondered why it mattered if the machine was taking special photos of my bones, like the man in the white coat had said, but I obliged and smiled. He sniggered. I added him to my hate list. Why did I let people make a fool out of me even when I knew that was happening?

I was returned to the corridor and recommenced my waiting.

My mind slipped backwards to Primary Four. We had to pick our favourite children's story and draw a picture of our favourite scene, label it, and then hang it on the designated space on the wall. This was a simple enough task for those sat close to me, and after a brief thinking period they started to work. I thought of the Emperor trusting his tailor and walking around in his new coat, and of Rumpelstiltskin or even Roald Dahl's *Witches*. I was fairly good at drawing, and I was confident I could create the required picture for any of these tales. But they all had the same problem: the picture had to be labelled.

Surely, I thought, if the scene was drawn correctly it would not require labelling; surely people would just know which story it was from. I thought about asking if the labelling was compulsory, but I knew that instructions already issued were non-negotiable. The picture would have to be labelled, so after much consideration I chose *Goldilocks and the Three Bears*, a story I disliked for its implausibility but nevertheless one I believed I could at least label correctly.

I set to work on the final chase scene, my favourite moment as it indicated the end of the story was near. My picture was okay, if a bit rushed, but it was nearly time to label and hang. In a moment of panic, I realised that in fact I was not sure how to spell "Goldie" or "bears," the first and last words of the title. How stupid of me. I should have written it down when I started, back when I knew how to spell it. Now I would have to ask two people – I could never trust just one person's answer as they could set me up to fail – or I would ask one person to write it down. I'd asked the folks at my table to help me with spelling in the past, which resulted in them bursting out laughing and informing the entire class that "Rhona doesn't know how to spell." This would be met with the usual ridicule from the entire class until the teacher quietened them down. Asking the kids at my table was not an option.

I got up and walked around the class, seeking a helpful face, and I found one. A girl had finished her drawing, labelled it, and was waiting for the command to pin it to the wall. I knelt down and complimented her on her drawing and said it was also one of my favourite stories. She asked what story I was doing. I described my drawing and as she was about to announce the title I said, "Don't say it! Someone will copy me, write it down," which she did on an envelope. I confirmed she was correct and returned to my seat. I carefully labelled my drawing and also sat waiting to be called to pin it up. When it was my turn, I duly presented my drawing with confidence and dropped the envelope close to the girl's desk as I walked past. The teacher said that the drawing was not up to my usual standards, but I did not care. It was labelled correctly, and that was what I had spent my time and effort achieving. The fact she did not comment on the labelling assured me that it was correct. We moved onto the next task, which was

Chapter 6

maths, so I could look forward to another few minutes free of embarrassment.

Suddenly, the teacher called the class' attention. The friendly girl was stood beside her holding the envelope. The teacher explained the envelope was addressed to the friendly girl's parents and that someone had taken it from her bag, where she had seemingly put it for safe keeping, and written on it. Would the person who did this please own up? There was silence. The teacher continued to request that the person who had taken this envelope from her bag and written on it be responsible for their own actions and confess; again, silence.

The teacher got more and more frustrated, and then the threats of the headmaster started to make their appearance. We were all past our Last Warning and were now in the territory of Very Last Warnings.

The teacher said it one more time, but this time she informed us what was written on the envelope: "Goldilocks and the Three Bears." My heart sank. Everyone in the class turned to me, but I sat like stone. I had to think fast. I couldn't say what had really happened – that the girl never actually put it in her bag, that I tricked her into writing it because I was unsure how to spell "Goldie" and "bears," that I could not ask the folks at my table for fear of them making fun of me. That she wrote it herself.

The girl was by now looking a little guilty, or maybe that was just my impression. The class remained certain that I was the guilty party, and the teacher turned her attention to me.

"Did you write 'Goldilocks and the Three Bears,' Rhona?"
"No."
"Are you sure?"
"Yes."
"Yes, you wrote it?"
"No, yes I am sure I did not write it, she wrote it herself."

"And please tell us why she would have written 'Goldilocks and the Three Bears.'"

"I don't know, you'd have to ask her."

This was a bad answer; if she did ask the girl and the girl explained, I could be found out for tricking the girl.

She turned to the once-friendly girl, who was my newest recruit to the list that was forming in my head. "Did you write this on the envelope?"

"No, Miss."

"Rhona, I'll ask you for the very last time, and then you will go to the headmaster's office. Did you write 'Goldilocks and the Three Bears?'"

There was no point prolonging this torment. I wanted it to be over, to be en route to see the headmaster, to be free from the class. "Yes."

"Why?"

"Don't know, Miss."

"Go and explain yourself to the headmaster."

There was a queue at the headmaster's office. The smelly kid in front of me was younger, and I guessed he was there because he had not washed in a week and the teacher could not stand the smell any longer. I was glad for the queue – it meant I was away from the class for longer. I was not sure what I was going to tell the headmaster, so the wait also allowed time for evaluating my options, thinking of the different reasons I could offer as an explanation as to why I wrote "Goldilocks and the Three Bears," which I'd not actually written.

The wait to see the headmaster felt the same as my current wait in the hospital corridor: a peaceful time to think and plan for the various options, any one of which may transpire when I reach the front of the queue.

7

My makeshift bed/trolley was placed in the hospital corridor once again, and my wait continued. Now that my bladder had been tended to, my wait had an uncertain conclusion.

Looking at the ceiling, with its striped lights and white tiles covered in little black dots, I started to count. I didn't know why I had to stop my mind drifting off to some better place, but I did know I needed to practise my concentration. I did not really know what concentration was, but I had to practise it. First I counted the lights, then the big white roof tiles, and finally the little black dots on the white tiles. I had no watch. I could see no clock. Time had no beginning, no passing, and no end.

A fellow in a white coat stopped by and confirmed that I had broken my tibia, then clarified by explaining that a tibia was a shinbone. Was I expected to know that? My mind burst into action. Tibia equals shinbone equals broken leg, or at least a broken shin. The tibia was not in our magnetic game "Operation," though the shinbone was.

I'd actually broken my leg, my shinbone, my tibia. There was an x-ray with me smiling to prove it. What a triumph.

I was delighted with myself. I'd not been red-sledged off

the hill for a bruised shin. I had stood on my broken tibia. I'd put my broken tibia into the front binding as I stamped down my heel to catch my back binding, and my tibia had reminded me of the fact that it was broken. I was relieved, as well as the most excited I could ever remember being. I'd not wasted everyone's time and efforts. I was not a hypochondriac demanding attention, at least not on this occasion. I'd never known anyone to break anything before; nobody in my family or even my class had ever had a broken bone.

I was told I would need plaster, which raised many questions. "How long will the plaster be on my leg? How big a plaster will it be? How much time will I need off school?" I rattled off my queries to the white-coated man – rudely, as I was leaving him no time to reply.

"Don't worry about school, they will be able to send work home."

I was not worried, I was excited. I was in Primary Six, and I hated it, even more than I hated other years. I hated the teacher. I hated my classmates. I hated my school. Having a doctor tell me that I had to stay home was the best possible news.

"School work at home?"

"Yes," he confirmed.

"Who would be my teacher?" I asked, praying he would not say my normal teacher would come to my house.

"'Maybe your mother, if she does not work."

"How long will I be in a plaster?" I enquired, wondering how long my mum could be my teacher at home.

"Maybe twelve weeks."

"Twelve weeks with mum being my teacher," I confirmed once more.

"We'll change your plaster in a while and you will be able to get a walking plaster, and then you will find moving about

Chapter 7

easier." I knew this would mark the point of returning to school.

"Have you got any pain?" he asked.

"No, I had a needle in the thigh."

"Yes, that was hours ago. We can give you more and keep you pain-free."

I consented. They rolled me over and the next needle was in my bottom. I still had a grey lead dot from the pencil-in-the-bottom incident of Primary Five, and I wondered if the doctor noticed it.

Like in most of my primary years, in Primary Five we had to queue at the teacher's desk to get our work marked. The first finished would be first up, which were always the clever kids. I used to aim to be halfway finished by the time the first kids were queuing; I seldom, if ever, made my goal. Eventually, the teacher would call for all those who had not finished, and that was my cue. As you stood waiting, you got to watch the kids in front of you get their work marked and see them getting shouted at for not moving past the question they got stuck on, or for not even trying, or for being slow, or because the teacher was now just shouting at everyone. Her response to my attempted work was a lottery. I knew I would get shouted at; the lottery part would be the reason, if a reason was even offered.

The "all those who have not finished yet" queue was particularly long one day. Like all the others in the queue, I leaned against a desk, despite being told by the teacher not to do so. What I did not realise was that the owner of the desk I was leaning on was the ringleader of the group who believed I was poison. He was the policeman's son, and I'm not sure how he had any friends. He wore the same thick-rimmed NHS glasses as I did, but mine were pink and his were blue. He did have thicker lenses in his; maybe that was his key to success, as the other kids always wanted to borrow his glasses. They would try to walk about in them, which was amusing to watch, although I was not supposed to be looking at him or his friends with my evil eyes.

He and another boy lived in the same direction from the school as I did. As we all left school at the same time, I inevitably would be walking just ahead or behind them. If they saw me behind them, they would jump off the pavement, walk on the road, and shout "poison!" The slower I walked, the slower they walked. If I stopped, they stopped. If I was ahead, I'd run. Ahead was better than behind, but they would run to keep up with me while shouting "poison, poison, poison." I'd more often than not lose my balance and fall, grazing my knees, as I twisted to see how close they were whilst keeping up my speed.

The owner of the desk noticed me leaning and quickly sharpened his pencil to a chorus of sniggers of encouragement. I was well used to sniggers and fairly well used to ignoring them, so I took no notice. He then proceeded to ram his newly-sharpened pencil into my behind. I screamed, the sniggers of encouragement now roaring into laughter. The teacher shouted and I cried, egging the laughter on even more.

I was sent to the headmaster's office, and the table of laughing children were silenced.

On route to the headmaster's office "to explain my unprovoked outburst" I pit-stopped in the toilet to examine what turned out to be a bleeding bottom, with the lead tip of the pencil lodged in my rear end.

I stood in the headmaster's office and once again explained why I had been sent. This time it was for screaming in class. I explained that the scream just came over me. That I was sorry. That I would not do it again. That I would apologise for disrupting the class from their studies. There was no point

Chapter 7

in explaining the pencil-meet-bottom story. I would not be showing the headmaster the proof, and after all, I did not want the headmaster or anyone else removing the deadly lead.

The bleeding had stopped before I got back to the bathroom on my return trip from the headmaster's office, although I did rather take my time on both my trip there and back. The bruise matured and faded, leaving a small grey lead dot of remembrance. As time passed it became clear that I'd need to return to biting the top of my pencil to reach the deadly dose for lead poisoning, as my teachers often warned me could occur.

The pencil-in-bottom incident was far more painful than the needle in the bottom for my broken tibia, so I settled back to counting dots and waiting.

8

I was aware of people moving around me in the hospital corridor. Screaming came and went. Babies, toddlers, and even a few parents sniffed and snorted. People told and retold their accident stories as families gathered. Sometime during the afternoon, it dawned on me that my family was not gathering, and my story was not being retold.

I was now recognizing the absence of my family as being unfamiliar and wrong in some way.

Time passed and there was movement of the patients around me, but I was not moving. The activity and business around me did not involve me. My mind rolled back; this had happened to me before.

Primary One had not been a great start to "the best years of my life." Every lunchtime we, the children, were sent to the bathroom to use the facilities and wash our hands before eating. Washing hands was something I was used to doing before any meal. My brothers and I would always claim our hands were clean, but we were still sent to wash our hands anyway. I was always amazed at how dark the water was that came off my pale white skin.

However, at school this routine was different. The other kids

Chapter 8

would tell the teacher if you did not go to the toilet, or at least go into a cubical and pretend to use to the toilet. They would report back as to who did or did not do what. I hated the whole stupid routine. I was never demanded to go to the toilet at home; we simply went to the bathroom when we needed to go. I had never had to excuse myself in the middle of a meal to go to the bathroom, nor had any member of my family, as it only takes fifteen minutes to eat dinner. At school, though, we were treated like prisoners and just told what to do, no choice, no discussion. The teacher was right and everyone else was wrong.

I was amazed at the kids who washed their hands before going to the toilet rather than after, but I did not care if they got bugs and died; in fact, I wished more of them would wash their hands first.

One day, as per usual, we were sent off to go to the toilet and wash our hands before lunch. I felt an urge but did not wish the entire class to know about it, so I sat on the toilet and lifted my feet up against the door and waited until it was quiet, then waited a little longer. I waited a long time. *Perfect*, I reassured myself, *I've spared myself from rounds of jokes*. I did what I had to do, then washed and dried my hands and headed back to the class.

To my surprise, the room was empty. I sat down at my desk and briefly wondered where everyone was – not that the emptiness bothered me. I started on the work that I had left, but after a while I recognised the empty classroom as odd, unfamiliar, and wrong in some way. I got up from my seat and went over to the window – no one was outside, everything was still and quiet. I wandered outside, an urge of panic slowly building inside me. There was no one. I walked round the school through the banned boy's side. Not a soul.

Had everyone left me alone? I had no idea, and strangely I

cared. Time had no beginning and no end. Was this the end of the world? If so, I hoped to enjoy whatever lay ahead. I sat down on the steps and watched the road to see if a car would pass, to see if there was anyone else left.

"Rhona?" a confused voice came from behind me.

"Yes," I calmly replied.

"What are you doing?" The voice was still confused.

"Sitting here to see how many are left." I turned to face the voice to make sure it was real. A woman was standing behind me, one I didn't recognize.

"Left where, Rhona?"

"Well, there is nobody in the school and nobody in the playgrounds. I've been right round, even went to the bit I'm not allowed to go. There's nobody, just me and now you."

"Why did you not go with the others?"

"I think I was in the toilet when they were taken."

"Taken where, Rhona?" The person was beginning to panic.

"I don't know, I was not there when they were taken," I said coolly.

"Who took them?"

"I don't know, I was not there at the time."

"What time is it, Rhona?"

"I don't know."

"Where do you think everyone is?" This person must have been getting frightened as she had started repeating her questions.

"I don't know."

"They are not in school?"

"No, I was in the class and then went to the gym hall."

"They are not playing?"

"No, we are in the playground and there is no one here."

"Where else could they be?"

Chapter 8

"I don't know."

"Where else do children go during school?"

"Home. Should I go home? Do you think someone will be there? I know the way home."

She was shaking her head, confused no doubt and more frightened than me.

"Are you hungry, Rhona?"

"No, not really."

"It might be lunchtime."

"Okay. If you are hungry, we can eat and then think about what to do."

We headed for the canteen across the road. It seemed a strange choice, as with no kids there would be no dinners, but we crossed the road together anyways. She made me look right, left, right, though it was obvious to me that there were no cars, and there was no one.

Once we got into the building, there was a horrible loud noise; it sounded like children. Then it dawned on me. She was one of the people who were gathering up the kids who escaped the first Rounding Up. I had been fooled. I had been caught. How silly of me. I knew I had been left alone, and I let myself be led into the trap.

We walked towards the door, the noise getting louder and more deafening with every step. The door opened to reveal the whole universe, or at least the whole school, eating their lunch. The headmaster came to greet me and my newfound friend.

"Where have you been Rhona?" he inquired.

"Nowhere," I replied.

"You must have been somewhere, lunchtime is nearly over."

I turned to locate the "friend" I had found, but she was gone. Was she ever real? She must have been real, we had a conversation. She asked questions. I answered them.

"Oh!" I mumbled as my mind started racing.
"Where have you been?" he demanded.
"I was looking for you."
"Well, we were here, so where were you looking?"
Why had she just disappeared? Should I even mention her? If she was another figment of my imagination, there would just be more questions. I decided to take the chance. "I looked in the playground, the class, and the hall. A lady found me, but when I looked around once we got here she was gone."
"Why did you not come with the others, Rhona?" he asked, not picking up on my mentioning of "her."
"When I came out of the toilet after washing my hands, they were all gone."
"We have been here for a long time, what about the rest of the time?"
"I sat in the class for a bit then started looking."
The kids were leaving in their neat queues, following each other like sheep – like lambs to the slaughter. A male support teacher came and said it was okay, and that he would wait and eat with me.

I felt so silly. Why had I forgotten it was lunchtime? Why had the lady done what she had done? If she knew it was lunchtime, why had she not just said so instead of making a fool out of me, letting me believe for a few brief moments that I had escaped everyone? How cruel of her! What a mean person. Whoever she was, I hoped I'd never see her again.

Someone got me lunch, someone who did not like me. It was ravioli in tomato sauce, and it looked so angry that it had been let out of a tin that I instantly wished it had not been. There were also potatoes and peas and a bowl of lumpy custard. It was all cold and horrible. I knew from that moment I was in the place where the bad people are sent to. They told me it was

Chapter 8

school, but I knew I was in prison. I ate the potatoes and the cold soft peas. I dreamed that the ravioli would just disappear – then I wished I would just disappear. *It's not fair,* I thought. *Life is not fair.*

The more the male tried to bargain with me to eat just one more mouthful, the closer I came to being physically sick. *It's not fair, it's not fair, it's not fair,* chanted through my mind. I could not swallow the custard. I still remember the feeling of the cold, lumpy texture, and the memory still makes me feel like throwing up. He told me I had to eat my lunch – there were starving children in Africa. *It's not fair, it's not fair, it's not fair.* Why can't I be a starving child in Africa? I wanted to go to Africa and be a starving child, with no school, lots of flies, no food, and a potbelly, like the children that were on the news.

Eventually he took me back to my class, where no one noticed my entrance. The afternoon was spent in confusion of what was real and reflection on what had happened and surreally what had not, when time stopped and everyone disappeared.

9

That strange feeling of aloneness, of being left by myself in a hospital corridor, disappeared as my father's head popped between my eyes and the black dots that I was still unsuccessfully trying to count. I was moved from the corridor to the plaster room. The nurse said it would be painful as they pulled and reshaped my leg. I was surprised to see that the nurse was holding the soft toy that usually sat on my pillow at home – I found out that my parents had brought it in for me, not her. She asked me all sorts of stupid questions.

"How old are you?"
"Eleven. Is that not on my chart?"
"Yes, which year of school are you in?"
"Six."
"Do you like school?"
"No!"
"What hobbies do you have?"
"Skiing."
"Any others?"
"Highland dancing, swimming."
"Have you got any brothers or sisters?"
"Two brothers."

Chapter 9

"Are they older or younger?"

"Older, both, they're okay. No cousins. One grandparent." I rattled on, not bothering to wait for the questions. Strangers' questions were always the same. Honestly, I'd prefer to be left alone, but to not answer these stupid questions was rude, and Mother did not want a rude child. "One rabbit, Thumper, two years old. A goldfish, Nike, three. My brother has a hamster, Eugenie, one. He had hamsters before this one. I want an Old English Sheepdog. He wants turtles. No, we did not get them for Christmas. I don't know what I want to be when I grow up. I play recorder, but not very well..."

Click. I heard a click. I think we all heard a click. It was then she stopped asking the stupid questions, the questions that she really did not care what the answers were. It was then the pulling stopped and the cool plaster started. It was then the nurse gave me back my toy and went to help the doctor with the rolls of cool, wet plaster. It was then she left me alone.

I was impressed with the plaster, which was applied in three main layers. I could see my toes peeking out the bottom and the top was mid-way up my thigh. It was heavy, but everyone told me I was excellent for wiggling my toes on demand. Every silver lining has its cloud, though, and my cloud was that I'd have to stay in hospital overnight. The doctor explained that I had been plastered too late and that it needed to set. I just wanted to go home.

"I broke my leg at one o'clock," I complained.

"We only got the plaster on at six-thirty," he replied.

"How is it my fault that you forgot about me in the corridor all afternoon?"

"We did not forget about you. Other children were screaming so we had to look after them quickly."

I wished I had screamed, I thought. I wanted to scream all the time, but I never did. I knew it was bad and the consequences of doing such a thing may never end, so I kept my scream to myself. I screamed in church. I screamed in assemblies. I screamed at the dinner table. I screamed when I woke up in the middle of the night. I ran around in circles and screamed, but I never made a sound, for I knew they would lock me away if I lived my screaming dream. But this afternoon would have been an acceptable time to scream. I had missed my chance.

10

The hospital ward was dark, with people huddled by each of the beds. It was 8:00 p.m. and visiting was over. My parents left, despite me pointing out that the other visitors showed no hint of leaving their little people in their strange hospital beds. My mother assured me that they would soon be asked to leave and promised to return first thing in the morning. Then, they were gone.

There were four beds in the room. The other parents did not move, and nobody came to chase them out.

The bed to my left had a small kid whose legs were both attached to a frame that hung above his bed. When he moved, the metal braces tied to his ankles hit off each other and disturbed everyone in the room, apart from him. The little girl opposite me just cried. Nothing appeared to be wrong with her, but she cried for ages after the boy with the braces woke her. The boy opposite him had one leg on a mountain of pillows a bit like me, apart from the fact my leg had slipped down off its mountain and my toes were resting on the metal sides designed to prevent people – or limbs, I suppose – from falling out of bed. I couldn't move my leg, it was too heavy to lift. I wished sleep would come and visit me, but sleep had deserted me just like my parents had.

The other adults slipped away after their child slipped into sleep. The parents of the little girl with nothing wrong with her were last to leave. Her mum came over to me.

"Do you want me to help lift your leg up again, or is it comfortable?"

"Can you help me lift it, please?"

"Of course."

She placed my leg back on its throne atop of the mountain of pillows with great care. I wondered what she did for a job, if anything, when she wasn't being mum to the crying girl.

"Thank you."

"You're most welcome, good night."

"What's the time please?"

"It's ten o'clock."

Thanks for answering the question I'd actually asked. We bid each other good night with a smile.

A nurse walked round a bit afterwards and ensured everyone was sleeping.

"You should be asleep," she said as she stopped by my bed.

"I can't sleep."

"Is your leg sore?"

"No."

"Can you wiggle your toes?"

I did so, and she confirmed the movement by shining the torch on them and then comparing them with the set of toes that did not belong to a broken leg.

"Try and get some sleep."

"What's the time?"

"Sleep time," she said as she left the room. That did not answer my question. Why can't people just answer the question that is asked?

I hated how adults always give an answer that does not answer

Chapter 10

the question at all; it's so very unhelpful. It's like they don't even listen but instead put words in your mouth just to finish the sentence they think you should be saying. I wondered, at what age do you get listened to? And when can the reply to their stupid answer be "well, that's great, but it does not really answer my question" without being rude and disrespectful?

Minutes later the boy moved, his braces clashed, the girl started sniffling, and my leg began its descent down its Everest pillow mountain. The boy settled and so did his braces, the girl's sniffles escalated to a cry, and the other fellow began sniffling. My toes slid closer towards the metal railing. The girl's cry quietened down and then stopped. The boy just stopped, as did my toes against the metal – they were cold. I waited, confident that the nurse would be coming back to reinstate my toes to their correct position, but she didn't return.

My toes were numb. I tried to wriggle them but they felt fat and clumsy and unwilling to obey my instructions. I looked for my call bell, and I could see it hanging on the wall far, far out of reach. I recommenced my wait.

I couldn't sleep, and my mind turned to dogs. I dearly wanted a dog. I wanted a Dulux paint dog, an Old English Sheepdog. Every Christmas I asked for a puppy, and every birthday I repeated my wish. I visited many dogs that my parents knew, including a big rough collie called Ben whom I visited many, many times. Ben lived next door, and I bargained nightly that I could go and see him if I did my homework. I would also go see Brandy, who was a mutt that lived behind us. Our other neighbour had springer spaniels, but I did not visit them often since Mrs Springer Spaniel had been my Primary Two teacher. But I did visit once when Mr Springer Spaniel invited me and Mrs Springer Spaniel was not there. They had a litter of suckling puppies that were hairless, with closed eyes. The puppies looked helpless. The puppies *were* helpless.

Calum was frightened of dogs, so we couldn't have a dog. I wondered why it was Calum who was frightened of dogs. He had never been bitten by a dog. I had, but I wasn't frightened of any of the dogs I visited, or any dog that I'd politely asked the owner if I could pat before doing so. I never patted dogs on their head. Ben's owner had showed me that dogs prefer to be stroked down their shoulders. I had practised stroking shoulders instead of patting heads on Rory, the rough collie who lived next door before Ben. Rory was elderly and his body needed rest so I did not know him very well, but he was the first dog I patted correctly. I loved Rory and Ben's owners; they never asked me about school, about teachers, about friends. They were my friends, and Ben was my best friend.

I did wonder why I had got bitten by that one dog, and how it was my fault. I had been visiting the house at the end of the road and there was a black lab asleep in its bed in a hallway. As I walked past it to go to the bathroom, the dog bit the back of my calf. The owner of the lab made me promise not to tell anyone. The dog had done this before to someone else, and I was informed that if I told anyone that he had bitten me he would be put down. His death would be because of me. We went into the bathroom and the owner bandaged up my leg after the bleeding stopped, telling me the story of the past bite and the consequences of telling anyone about this one.

I went home and curled into bed. Mum came several times as I was trying to sleep. My leg was sore so I was crying, but I couldn't tell her why. I didn't want the dog to be killed because of me. I simply wouldn't visit it again.

Mum wouldn't leave though. She said she knew something

Chapter 10

was wrong. But something was wrong every day that I walked to school in tears, yet she left me then.

My leg was too sore to ignore. I made her promise not to report the dog as I did not want him to be destroyed, but I told her that he bit me. She unbandaged my leg, which actually relieved some of the pain. She then called a doctor, who didn't have to come because my shots were up to date and I didn't need a booster.

There was lots of talk about how dogs don't bite for no reason and that I must have kicked it or its bed, which I hadn't, but I said that maybe I hit the bed by accident. I did not tell them that the dog had done the same thing to someone else. I was at fault for kicking the bed, even though I never touched it.

Dad used to say, "Always let sleeping dogs lie." He said it as an answer to my questions about his life and childhood, using it to hide his meaning. But maybe this meaning did not have to be hidden. It could be best practice to never wake a dog that is sleeping. Dogs must have nightmares too; sometimes they must wake up protecting themselves in the only way they can, by biting. The black lab was not destroyed, I did not visit him again, and I developed four white dots on the back of my calf.

I continued to visit Ben and Bilbo the cat, Ben's housemate, along with their guardians. The house was always fun, and silliness filled every visit. Mr Bilbo would eat Ben's chocolate drops and make farting noises every time I pulled his finger. Adults acting inappropriately was such a different experience from my own always-serious household, where homework will take up the entire evening if homework wants.

Bilbo was the only cat I visited, and in reality I was actually there to see Ben. Once when I was holding Bilbo, he started nipping me in the inner side of my elbow. I wasn't sure if Bilbo was actually biting as it was far less painful than the leg bite, so I gave him to Mrs Bilbo who shouted "Ow!" and dropped Bilbo within seconds. I learned that dog bites are far sorer than cat bites.

Every Christmas I gave Ben and Bilbo presents. In fact, I gave all the dogs I visited presents, but I really loved Ben. I wanted a Ben of my own. My dog's bed would not be in a hallway. My dog would be free to run and chase rabbits in its dreams, and it would be safe when it woke up from a nightmare where it had to fight to survive. I had never, and would never, wake a sleeping dog.

11

The hospital ward clock was noisy. I could hear it ticking but could not work out the time. At first I thought it clicked every fifteen minutes, but I heard nine sets of clicks and no hour chime.

The band tightening around my arm awakened me from my daze. It had done the same before, and I knew it would then bleep and a score would appear on the screen. I pulled the cuff off my arm and got a score of 000/000, a score below even my worst one. The machine started beeping as I had hoped, although far louder and in a different tune than I'd expected. The boy moved and set off his braces and the little girl started crying, who again set off the little boy. Someone would have to come now.

As I heard the steps getting closer, I started getting apprehensive. I had caused this ruckus by pulling off the cuff. I had made the machine go mad. I had made the boy move, the girl cry, and the boy sniffle. It was entirely my fault. Everyone had been sleeping peacefully, and just because I could not sleep I had to disturb everyone else. I was so selfish. I was going to get into big trouble. I wished I had not pulled the cuff off. My mother was right, I really do need to think more about what my actions do to other people. My parents would be mad if they found out I caused all this on purpose. I wished I could get the cuff back on and pretend to be asleep. Pretend I'd not disturbed everyone. Pretend not to be bad.

"We need to check your blood pressure, Rhona," the nurse said as she replaced a cuff, her voice a gentle whisper that assured me I was not in trouble.

"My foot slipped down and my toes are cold, very cold, and they won't move," I announced.

"Where is your sock?" she asked as she switched on my bed light.

"I don't think I had one."

"Why did you not call?" she asked, lifting my leg to the Everest summit again.

"Because I could not reach my bell."

The machine went bleep as she was pinning my bell to my sheet by my shoulder.

"Will you have a big drink for me, Rhona?"

"Yes, I'm hungry, I don't know when I last had food."

"It would have been supper time last night."

"No, the trays were getting collected when I arrived here."

"Lunch yesterday?"

"No, I fell skiing as we were going for lunch."

"What would you like to eat?"

"Pizza."

"What about some toast?"

"Okay."

"Butter on top?"

"I don't like butter, raspberry jam?"

"I'll see what I can do. Hot milk or cold milk?"

"I don't like milk, only in hot chocolate with lots of water."

"Okay, I'll see what I can do."

Chapter 11

She left, and I thought of my Grandma's jam. She made the best raspberry jam in the whole world. Not that I've tasted all the raspberry jam in the world, but hers was yummy and I couldn't imagine anything else being tastier. There was always raspberry jam and pancakes when we visited the farm to see the McKenzies.

My mother was a McKenzie before she was Macdonald. Her father was a master farmer and butcher, her mother a doting parent of five children. My mother was also the youngest, like me. Her only sister, the eldest child, had left home at seventeen to train to be a nurse. My mother was five when she left, and so memories of her sister are limited to holiday time. The children between were boys, the middle of whom was granted rest from this world at two years, two months due to something called meningitis. Mother's father, my grandfather, was also dead. He had died three days after a heart attack at sixty-six years old; my mother was twenty-one and unmarried at the time of his death.

My father's life was a far sadder story, and one that I was far more interested in. Sadly, it was one that Dad did not freely share. He was happier with sayings like "the past is the past, let it be just that" and "don't look too hard, you never know what you will find." These repeated responses to my repeated questions just made me more determined to find out his history, the story he was unwilling to share.

The Macdonalds were complicated; it was slow progress to uncover the facts, and even slower progress to fill in the gaps. So far, I knew that I had two aunties on my dad's side, his two older sisters. He was the only boy. Both his parents were dead. He had been born in Dulnain Bridge, a village three miles from Grantown. He moved to Glasgow following his parents death to live with an aunt that he had never met.

The nurse returned with a sock and two blankets, one of which she put over the metal railing and the other she put over me. Then she fetched some toast and strawberry jam and hot chocolate. Strawberry jam was not raspberry jam, but it is better than apricot jam. The hot chocolate was not very chocolaty, but it wasn't too milky either and it did not have the horrible skin on top. I gulped it all down. She came back one more time to blow up the cuff on my arm and asked me to wiggle my toes, which were now responding to requests. After the machine went beep, she ensured I had my bell and switched off my light. She said she would check on me in a bit and left the room.

My mind drifted back to my family. The only grandparent I had ever met – Grandma McKenzie – had died from a mixture of old age and cancer just as the weather was getting colder last year, signalling the end of the raspberry jam era. I wasn't allowed to go to the funeral as I wasn't mature enough, but I did get the day off school which I was very happy about. I liked days off school. I plotted and scammed as many days off as I could from as far back as I could remember.

My Primary Two school teacher turned out to be my imaginary friend that I'd met in the playground when I thought everyone had disappeared the year before, the day I took too long in the bathroom and forgot about lunch. She was the one who played along with my belief that everyone had vanished out of my life. She was the one who led me back to them. She was the one who left me to explain my absence alone, and now here she was, the one who would teach me for a whole year. I already knew she could not be trusted, and she already knew I was an idiot. I knew Primary Two was going to be a long year.

Wednesday morning was the most hopeful day of Primary Two. The least feared. The day which would make or break the rest of the week. On Wednesday mornings I was excited,

Chapter 11

nervous, and scared. If I timed things right, Wednesday was the last day of the school week for me.

I only had to survive until morning break. It was fairly easy to ignore the teacher for the first few hours as she was usually busy attending and adorning the clever kids with their new tasks; us daft ones would still be redoing yesterday's tasks till lunch. It was always the same, but not on Wednesday mornings.

Wednesday break meant only one thing to me: time to eat the soap in the toilets.

The teacher herself gave me the idea of eating soap. I'd never have thought of it myself, but they would come into class now and then and warn us not to drink water out of the taps in the bathroom as someone has pushed soap up the inside and it would make us ill. Of course, I was more than willing to test the theory. I was caught once drinking from the forbidden tap, and that's when I realised that I did not have to wait for someone else to push soap into the tap. I didn't even have to push the soap in myself. All I had to do was get some of the soap and sit in cubicle, eating my morning playtime snack.

On good Wednesdays, after my consumption of soap, I would throw up over my work in class. This was a double triumph: not only had I thrown up, but I had successfully done it over my yet-to-be-corrected work. I would be told that I should have said that I was feeling ill, to which I would say I had told my mum before coming to school. Mum would be summoned to collect me, and I'd be back in the security of my bed by lunchtime.

Before I discovered this ploy, I had taken to "catching" whatever my brothers had fallen ill with. If they were off school, then I needed to be off school as well. Once, Mother had taken them to the doctor as they had been ill for ages, so she announced that I too would have to go to the doctor when I "fell ill." To say that I suddenly felt better would make me a hypochondriac, so I had to follow though and put up no protest about going to the doctor. The appointment was made for the next day, so at least that meant one day off school before the doctor found me out for lying.

We arrived at the doctor's odd-smelling clinic. I'd asked on a previous trip what the smell was and been told the smell was "clean." I'd also asked if our house was clean and was told yes, but our house did not smell the same sort of clean. Then I was informed not to be silly and that there were different types of clean. Our house was clean and so was the doctor's clinic, but they smelt nothing alike whatsoever. I had a notion that both could not be clean. My hands were either clean or dirty, my room was either clean or dirty, my teeth were either clean or dirty. As I pondered this, trying to work out if there was something else other than clean or dirty, I recalled mother sometimes mentioned "better" in relation to clean, so maybe better was another state of clean.

After waiting in the clean-smelling waiting room, my name was called and mother started moving towards the voice. I followed nervously, sure that the clever doctor would work out that I had been lying to get off school. My mother talked and I sat quietly, waiting to be spoken to before interrupting. The doctor turned to me.

"So Rhona, your mum says you have a headache?"
"Yes."
"Where about is it?" he inquired.

What did he just say? My mind was racing off. Had he not sung the song about the parts of the body being connected – the neck bone connected to the head bone, and so on? Had he not played Operation with the tweezers and the buzzer if you touched the metal while removing the bits of the body?

Chapter 11

How could he not know where your head was? Was he even a doctor? Should he not have learned it properly and not had to rely on silly kids' songs and games?

"It's in my head," I said, confident that I'd gotten the latest question correct.

"Oh yes, of course, how silly of me."

My mother sat there as if he had said nothing idiotic. He might have been a doctor, but I now knew I could not believe anything he said. He was a fool, a clown, who didn't know where a headache was. How on earth was I meant to believe his diagnosis? I was reassured he'd never find out I was making it up.

He said he would look in my head and stuck something in my ear that moments later went bleep. The thing he stuck in my ear was a proper temperature taker, better than the one we had at home that I would put on my hot water bottle. He said, "Well, everything's fine in there."

This guy was a joke. Not only did he take my temperature with a machine he put in my ear and thought he was looking inside my head, but he said everything was fine in there. This was utter rubbish, since there was something very wrong with my head. How nice it would be if someone could look into my head and fix me. Fix my head. Make me normal. But I knew it was not going to be this guy.

There were more questions, all yes or no answers. Like being sick, feeling sick, feeling hot, having sore joints. He strangely asked some of the questions more than once. It could be that he had short-term memory loss, but I couldn't trust him. I wondered if he was just playing with me, trying to make me the fool. Trying to be sneaky and catch me out. I knew what I had said yes and no to, though, and I knew where a headache would be.

He didn't catch me out. He said that I likely had the same as whatever Calum and Evan had and suggested rest and time off school. He was talking to mother now so I did not have to answer. I was silently overjoyed. Within thirty minutes I was back in my bed, safe with my dreams, alone and unbothered once again.

When I did successfully make myself sick, or successfully pretend I caught my brothers' sickness, I would spend a glorious Wednesday afternoon alone with my thoughts and my dreams of escaping and wondering how best to do it. I would then claim ongoing illness and barely eat any dinner on Wednesday evening, and I was never recovered by Thursday morning and therefore scored another day off. Mother did not want to pack me off to school just in case the vomit returned and she was asked again if she knew of my illness before sending me.

Everyone knew that Friday was not a real day at school. I would still feel ill and Mum would allow me to stay at home but made me promise I would go to school without a fuss on Monday, with no illness and no nuisance.

I didn't mean to, but every Monday morning I would break my promise. I would refuse to get out of bed. Refuse to eat anything. Refuse to get dressed. Refuse to do my teeth. Refuse to go to school. I'd tell Mum that I hated school. That I couldn't do anything they asked me to do. That I hated her for making me go. That if she loved me, she would not make me go. That they were mean to me and picked on me. She would remind me of my promise and that I was being bad.

I was told I would be late. I didn't care. I didn't care that my brothers had left ages ago. My mother would have to dress me as I played at being paralysed. If she left me to do something else, I'd undress and get back into the safety of bed and she would have to dress me again. Every day she dressed me, often

Chapter 11

dressed me more than once. Every day I cried. She would coax and plead me to eat something, to do my teeth, to go to school, and I never wanted to do any of it. I hated school. They were mean to me; the kids, the teachers, all of them.

Mother used to say that if I didn't go to school, they would take her away. It was the law that I went to school. By allowing me to stay off school, I was making her break the law, making her a criminal, and she would be locked up and then we would have no mother to look after us. Is that what I wanted, she would ask? For "them" to take her away?

I understood that I had to go to school, but every day for years I would cry. I never ran out of tears. I would walk past one house and then turn back, crying. I would arrive home and have to blow my nose and be sent off to school. I would turn back so many times, each time walking a little further. Each retreat was greeted with a clean tissue and another send off. Sometimes she would be cross at me for wasting so much time, sometimes she would be quiet, but she always sent me off again. Sometimes she would walk part of the way with me, but I would just follow her home when she turned back towards safety. I didn't want to go. I hated it. I hated them. They hated me.

It could take over an hour to get me through the classroom door. It took ten minutes for me to get home after school ended.

As the weeks went by, I discovered that I was having to eat more and more soap for it to have any visible effect. It was no use just feeling ill – you don't get sent home from school for not feeling well, you have to actually be sick. Sadly, the soap lost its effect; it was good while it lasted though, and it got me through Primary Two.

I was hopeful that my broken leg would give me a lifeline through Primary Six.

12

Morning arrived in the hospital ward and someone I did not recognize woke me. Not the person who had helped me and fed me during the night; I would never see her again. My machine with the cuff had also gone.

"It's time to get up and have a shower," the voice said, sounding a little annoyed at me although I did not know why. Then again, frequently I did not know why adults were annoyed at me.

"What's the time?" I enquired, completely aware I'd done the thing my mother hated – changed the subject.

"Five thirty."

What sort of five thirty, I wondered? Surely I'd not slept all day, but surely it's not five thirty in the middle of the night? The ward lights were on, so I wasn't sure; both five thirties looked the same this time of year. But, concentrating on her first statement, did she say shower?

"How can I have a shower with this?" I asked while nodding at my leg, surprisingly still in place on its summit of importance.

"The same as you did yesterday."

"I didn't have a broken leg this time yesterday," I replied, taking the chance that I'd not slept all day.

Chapter 12

"Oh, I'll get you a basin then."

My question was answered. It was five thirty in the morning, when everyone I knew would be asleep. Evan's hamster would be the only one up, going round and round and round in his wheel. The hamster would lick off the oil or butter as fast as Father could get it on his ever-squeaky wheel. The little thing seemed to love running, putting all his efforts into the activity and getting nowhere. He never got ahead, he just went round and round in circles. Did he know it got him nowhere? He had no spectators telling him to try harder, telling him he could do better with more effort. No one lied to him. Did he really like running? When he ran very fast he could get half way up the height of his wheel, and when he stopped there was so much momentum that he would do a loop and sometimes two backwards as a passenger. Maybe he just took enjoyment in disturbing the peace? The squeak…squeak…squeak of his oil-deprived wheel would echo through the house, reminding us that not only was the hamster alive but so too was the person hearing the squeak…squeak…squeak.

By 6:00 a.m., the basin had come and gone. I knocked my plaster to test it; it was hard. I was ready for my parents to arrive and take me home.

At 6:30 a.m., the little crying girl got out of bed and walked out of the ward, confirming that nothing was wrong with her. The boy hopped out on a pair of crutches and then duly hopped back. The boy in braces crashed and bashed them together behind curtains as if he were trying to escape. They all knew the routine. Their parents returned, the last to leave being the first to arrive.

By 7:30 a.m., the only empty chairs were beside my bed. I felt lost, abandoned, scared, and very much alone, far more so than the previous afternoon.

Breakfast arrived at 8:00 a.m. I opened each container in turn hoping to find something edible, and each container failed me. In fact, each was worse than the last. No wonder I never ate breakfast. The orange juice was sour. The cornflakes had been drowned in milk far too long ago, so the flakes were mush. On the few times I would eat breakfast, I had my cornflakes in the bowl and my milk in a glass by the side. I would slowly eat the cornflakes and seldom touch the milk. There was bread with butter on one side. Not even toast, just bread. I left the containers alone so they might think about what they had done. I would miss breakfast, but it did not matter; my parents would be in the hospital lift coming to collect me.

I remember being left in some sort of nursery once. I remember there being rows and rows of cots. I remember only wearing a nappy. I remember standing at the end of my allotted cot and crying. I remember that no one came to soothe my cries. I don't remember for how long or where I was left in those rows of cots, but I did remember it.

I'd asked Mother once where she left me. She told me I was being silly – that I was never left, that I was always loved, that my cries were always answered. I was certain it had happened. Mother was certain it hadn't.

It was bit like school, the waiting, but better than school since nobody bothered me or made fun out of me. My stomach was uneasy, though. I felt that something was wrong.

At 9:30 a.m., a woman armed with crutches and no broken leg approached my bed. "I'm Physiotherapist," she said.

"Hi, I'm Rhona," I replied. I guessed she actually had a real name, but I silently chuckled at her introduction. At the same time, I knew that I very likely had made myself not hear the "a" in the middle of her claim. No one could be called Physiotherapist.

Chapter 12

I edged out of bed with help and got upright. The crutches were adjusted to fit me. They were uncomfortable and rubbing under my arms, but of course I was doing it wrong. I had to take my weight on my hands, not my underarms. Miss Physiotherapist made them shorter so I could no longer cheat. I practised. I had to learn how to hop about like the little boy before they would let me go home.

Learning how to hop about on crutches was not my biggest concern. My biggest concern was how I would get home if my parents did not show. I needed clothes. I needed a car. I needed a driver. Where were they?

By 10:00 a.m., I was deemed safe on my crutches. Did that mean I passed? Deemed, what was that? It sounded like a pass!

I was now able to hop out to the clock to confirm the time. The clock said 10:30 a.m., then 11:00 a.m. the next time I checked.

Maybe they were dead. Maybe they had had a car accident while racing to see me first thing. Maybe they were lying in the corridor where I was yesterday. My brothers would not know where I was. They wouldn't look after me if my parents were dead, they weren't old enough. They would blame me for their deaths. After all, I was the reason Mum and Dad were making the journey to Inverness on such bad roads. If I was really lucky, I would not get blamed for their deaths. Maybe it could be an accident. A bit like me: a tragic accident! But no, I'm sure it would be my fault, and I'd have to live with myself.

"Live with yourself." That was something my mother always threatened but I never quite understood. Doesn't everyone have to live with themselves? When I suggested this to her, I was told I was being cheeky again. Living with myself seemed like something I could do though. In fact, what I wanted to learn was how *not* to live with myself.

If my parents were dead, what would happen to me? Would I have to go and live with an aunt that I'd never met, like my father had? It would have to be Auntie Helen, who lived in Australia. My mind wandered to happy, hopeful thoughts of getting a chance to start again. I promised myself I would be well behaved and try really, really hard at school. I would not cause trouble, or lie, or pretend. Yes, I would be good for Auntie Helen in Australia.

But really, what sort of child was I, wishing her parents dead just so she might have a better life? They were right, I was selfish, I did only think of myself. I was a terrible person, really terrible, for thinking such dreadful thoughts. Who in their right mind would wish their parents dead? I was a bad child, ungrateful for everything everyone had ever done for me.

I had wished myself dead for many years, like my parents probably were now. Somewhere in my past, I had collected a little canister of crystals that stated "DO NOT EAT" in big, red, printed lettering. I'd collected it years ago – well, I actually took it without asking permission, so truly I'd stolen it from my mother's new handbag. I kept it thinking it was my insurance, my guarantee. I kept the little canister hidden in my room, somewhat comforted by the knowledge that whenever I chose to eat the contents, the failure of my miserable life would be over. I thought many, many times about swallowing them; I'd fall asleep with it in my hand and wake up with it in my hand.

The fear of them not actually being poisonous prevented me from consuming them. If I was to awaken in hospital after eating the packet there would be a never-ending list of questions to answer, and I would have failed at yet one more thing. Every night I'd pray I'd be one of the lucky people who just slipped away in their sleep, and every morning I awoke I'd wish my teacher dead.

Chapter 12

There was one teacher, my Primary Six teacher, that I did not have the vocabulary for what I wished for her. She was simply the purest form of evil I had ever encountered. She made me suffer, took joy in my suffering, and did not even try to hide her joy. An evil smile would sweep her face every time tears rolled down mine.

With this teacher, Wednesdays once again became a lifesaver. The evil teacher went to teach music on Wednesday afternoons, and so we were taught by the headmaster. I liked the headmaster. He talked a lot and we listened, answering together when required. This was the sort of answering I liked; no one noticed that although my lips moved, I did not make any noise. I never said the wrong answer, but I always answered.

I never thought the headmaster was a teacher, but rather an entertainer. He never flaunted his knowledge like all the others did. He didn't boast about the stuff he knew and that we, or at least I, did not. He never appeared to feel the need or urge to make anyone cry. He seemed happy talking, and I was more than happy to listen. He was a gentle entertainer in the classroom I so hated, but I also knew he was a man of position.

I would see him in church at the weekend too. He would read the bible, and everyone would listen in silence. He would pronounce unpronounceable words perfectly, words I could only dream of pronouncing, let along comprehending. He spoke well, whether he was speaking in church, chatting at the blackboard, or correcting the naughty children that had been sent to him yet again.

He was always poised and ready to deal with me and the other naughty children that were sent out of their class. Sometimes there was a queue to see him, but he was not an angry man. He never shouted at me on any of my visits to him. I often wondered if he was really suited to sorting out us naughty children.

The first Wednesday the Entertainer Headmaster taught us, he came in and pinned a map of the world on the blackboard. He talked about the world – the different countries, different people, different lives, different animals – and I listened intently.

He was certainly a man of knowledge; he knew a great many things about the world outside our sleepy little town. He knew a lot about Iraq and Iran. They were neighbours but did not like each other, and the headmaster predicted their dislike for each other would turn into war. I listened extra carefully when he spoke of Iraq and Iran and this war he knew was coming.

I rather liked the idea of war, of death and destruction, of everyone equal in their poverty or ignorance. I asked if he thought it would be a world war or just a little local war. He said it would start small and grow quickly, and he thought it may expand into a world war. I also quizzed him for a start date, but he just said "soon." I asked what that meant – was soon days, weeks, or years away? He just said soon.

This knowledge gave me hope; maybe the answer to my prayers was closer than I dared to dream. If this war started and grew into a world war, they – Iraq or Iran or both – would bomb London like in the last war. We knew the Germans missed a lot of their targets with their bombs; maybe this time, one would hit our sleepy little town. I knew it was unlikely, given the distance between London and our town, but the Royal Air Force did have stations nearby that the pilots used to practise all the time. Maybe Iraq or Iran would bomb the training stations; maybe they would miss the training stations.

On another World Map Wednesday, the headmaster asked us in turn to point to where we would each like to live and say why. Lots of kids pointed to our sleepy little town, which was not actually marked on the map, and said it was the greatest place on earth because it's where their mums, dads, brothers,

Chapter 12

sisters, and friends were. When it was my turn, I thought about doing the same, just pointing to where everyone else had pointed and saying that I loved my mum and dad, but when stood at the map I pointed to the bottom right of a big island down on the bottom right of the map and then looked at him.

"Australia, Rhona?" he said.

"If that's Australia, then yes, I'd like to live there," I replied.

"And why is that Rhona?" he asked.

"Because it is far away from here," I stated.

"That is true. Thank you, Rhona. Next please," he said, acknowledging my correct answer.

I made my announcement about my chosen island to my family that evening. I had thought they would be sad to see me go or maybe even try and talk me out of it, but almost the opposite occurred. My mother told me about Auntie Helen in Sydney. My father said it was a wonderful and huge place, very hot with snakes. On further questioning, I found out neither had ever been. My brother asked if he could help me pack, a comment which was met with a slap round the head from Mum and a giggle from me. My other brother did not waste his time by commenting or even acknowledging my decision.

Yes, if my parents were dead, I'd live with Auntie Helen in Australia. It would be big and hot and very far away from here.

13

As it turns out, my parents were not dead; they arrived at 1:45 p.m. I tried not to be disappointed, but I was. I had been waiting for five and three quarter hours. I had thought they were dead. I had hoped they were dead; I'd started my second chance at life in Australia. Deep down, I knew these thoughts made me a bad person, so I pretended these thoughts had not happened. I wouldn't tell anyone about these thoughts. Not everyone needed to know what an awful a person I was for thinking such thoughts, only me. I had to live with myself and my thoughts every single day, day after day after day.

The roads had been treacherous, apparently, but I was told visiting hours started at 2:00 p.m. so they were, in fact, early. That I should be thankful that they were early. That I was lucky they were early. That the other mother who arrived to see her child before breakfast was breaking the rules. I did not have to be told again that breaking rules was bad or that the rules were set for a reason. No one ever told you the reason though, so I suppose the reason did not matter. Rules were rules, and they had to be observed and respected. I wondered who made up the rules.

I tried to reassure myself that my parents were fifteen minutes

Chapter 13

early, and that they loved me. After all, they had to wait until the local shop opened at 11:00 a.m. to get the raspberry fizzy drink I had apparently requested the day before. It was Easter Sunday after all. What that had to do with it, I did not bother asking. Mother stated that the shops did not open until 11:00 a.m. on Easter Sunday. I never had any way of verifying her claim, or what any adult said, so as usual my only choice was to accept it, which means I didn't really have a choice at all. If I ever questioned whatever statement had just been made, I was reminded that questioning what an adult was saying was rude; it was the same as interrupting.

The horrible dentist in our town was another example of this. I was unimpressed by the dentist's own teeth, which were yellow with big brown marks. I wondered if he had previously attempted a career as a boxer, which could possibly explain why he had so few teeth himself.

I put the argument to my parents, how could he tell me that my teeth were bad, uncared for, out of alignment? At least I had teeth. Did he know what a mirror was for? Did he know what a dentist was meant to do? He had stolen my mother's front teeth when she was first pregnant. The baby needed the calcium, but only the first baby; she did not have to surrender any teeth during her second and third pregnancies. It made no sense to me, but I was being disrespectful of the man's skill by asking.

He was the only dentist in the town, though, so every six months I went to see the yellow-toothed monster. He was just like the teachers: if they were shouting at one kid and you were next in line, it almost guaranteed you would get shouted at as well. Here, if the drill was out, it never went away.

On the better days he would talk in code, muttering to himself as he rammed some spiky tool into selected teeth and pulled while telling me to brush better. On not so good days, the spiky tool would get jammed so far into my tooth that it was embedded in the jaw, if not my tonsils. On those days he'd fill my mouth with cotton wool and ask me how school was, informing me that these were the best years of my life.

He warned me that I had to stop sucking my thumb, threatening that I would end up with false teeth. Now, this was the first and last sensible thing this dentist ever said to me. If I had false teeth, then they could go and see him for their six-month check-ups while my nerves were left unscathed. I would not have to continue to rub my mouth ulcers and make them bleed twice a day. I would not have to look at his teeth and could save myself the lectures about the importance of brushing and how I only had ulcers because I did not brush. I was ready to sign up. But, as I should have expected, this was not actually on offer to me; he was going to take pleasure in collecting his government money, paid for seeing me every six months until I was sixteen.

I was not allowed to question the dentist, and I was not allowed to question my parents. Had I asked for the raspberry fizzy drink the day before? It was possible. I knew I liked the drink, but I also knew I was not allowed it. I also liked Daley Thompson Lucozades but only got those when I was ill. A broken leg was not ill, so I might have taken the opportunity of a broken tibia to see if I could get some raspberry fizzy drink. My brothers called it "milking it," something I'd done many times – making use of the current situation to get something else I wanted.

The doctor came at the same time as the lunch tray; one that was a waste of time. The doctor watched me on my crutches, asked about steps and bathrooms in our house, and declared me fit to go home providing that I returned to see him in clinic in a few weeks.

Chapter 13

Somebody got a wheelchair for me as I was too wobbly with my crutches to get all the way to the car. I waved a goodbye/thank you/I love you/can you be my mum to the girl's mum who was attentively helping her daughter eat a lunch that she had brought in, as – like me – her daughter had pushed away her lunch tray.

Dad had taken the big car, but it turned out to be surprisingly small. My plaster and I ended up on the back seat, sat at an angle, and the journey home commenced. My new attachment was aching and heavy. I tried to explain my last twenty-four hours, my feeling of abandonment, but I was told I was being silly and was just frightened because I'd broken my leg. I looked out the window and hoped we would be involved in a terrible car crash, and that I would die.

As we drove, I learned that Father had been spraying the motorbike and sidecar the day I broke my leg, a task he took great pride in doing yearly. The outfit was always red, white, and blue, with "Wm Macdonald, Coachbuilders" across the side as a sponsor. We had gone to see the motorbike races many times: Brands Hatch, Donnington, Silverstone, Sneddon. I'd fallen asleep right by the Isle of Man TT track once, not that I remembered doing this. I don't even remember being on the Isle of Man. I don't remember being at any of the tracks. I can recall the zoom noise, and there are photos of me by tracks with the name and year written on the back of the photo. There's a photo of me curled up on a tartan blanket with bikes whizzing past me in the background – that one was the Isle of Man TT. So, I've been there.

Father told everyone that I'd fallen asleep by the track. Somehow, he saw this as an unbelievable achievement, something he considered impossible. I was the only one in my family able to do this; everyone else watched the bikes go round and round and round. I was unconvinced this was notable achievement as it came without effort or pain. I fell asleep most nights in bed – did he not? Achievement was both painful and exhausting. I let him tell everyone about this almost impossible achievement that I had managed, but I knew it was nothing and he was just lying so that I could feel good about something. He must have thought it was good for my confidence, but truthfully I thought he could have picked something better to herald than the fact I'd fallen asleep.

That year – the year I achieved falling asleep at the Isle of Man TT – the boys driving the outfit came second. When Dad was talking to them later he said, "Well done lads, another mark of failure." Dad laughed, and one of the boys said, "Sorry Willie, we'll try harder." I'd never considered second place a mark of failure, it was actually quite the opposite to me, but I tried not to worry about it. I'd never be second anyway, so it was not something I needed to concern myself with.

Father also watched motor racing on TV; he said he watched to see what damage he had to repair before they raced again. Sometimes he did this with his eyes closed. He always watched the news with his eyes closed. He said he liked to rest his eyes after working all day.

Mother blamed him for their lateness at the hospital on the day I broke my leg. I was reminded that "once your father starts spraying, he can't stop or he'll have to start again." Father said, "Your mother said you were fine when she saw you in Aviemore," and that he could stop and would have stopped if I'd asked. I never got the chance to ask. It didn't matter, though, because I was more upset about them being over five hours late this morning, or fifteen minutes early as they claimed. I was tired and longed to get home to the safety of my bed.

The journey was not long and treacherous – the conditions

must have dramatically improved since my parents had driven to get me. I got into my beloved bed, pleased with the plaster of Paris on my leg. My mind was free to drift, and I found myself wondering where I fit into my life, into my family.

My mother was a well-respected lady within our town. She was Akela in the Cub Scouts, having joined the organisation when Evan did not like Cubs and refused to go and stayed there long after he had outgrown it. She was also on many charity committees, including Cancer Relief – not to be confused with Cancer Research, as she believed research should be government-funded. She was treasurer of this charity because she was excellent at maths, or was it because she was competent at maths and nobody else wanted the responsibility? Either way, I could have done worse than becoming like my mother. She was admired and appreciated. So, I joined in her activities where I could, hoping that this would help me fit in with the world around me.

Many times I sat in church in my Sunday best with Mother, the minister trying his hardest to explain unfathomable words and stories, and I screamed my lungs out in silence. I would never become my mother if I permitted my scream to come out. Instead of screaming, I continued to pour coffee and tea at coffee mornings. I was polite. I answered questions with the appropriate correct answers, the answers they wanted to hear. Never the truth; no one liked it when I spoke the actual truth. I explained what year I was in and that yes, I did enjoy school. They all agreed that my school years were the best years of my life, and that my mother must be very proud of me.

Once I was home with my broken leg, Mother rushed around fussing so that I had everything within arm's reach. My brothers informed the world that I was milking it for as much as I could get. Was that not the responsibility of an ill child though? Not that I was technically ill. All I looked forward to was being off school, which was the sorest of all points for my brothers to swallow. They already thought I was granted far too much time off school as it was.

My broken leg was a gift. I knew I was not going to make it through Primary Six alive otherwise, but this time away from school would help me finish this year and get onto the final lap of Primary Seven.

14

Work was sent home from school to be completed in the company of my broken tibia, most of which was painless to do. However, it was suggested that I repeat Primary Six. They wanted to hold me back as I'd missed a lot of work. I was below average in my reading, below average in my writing, below average in my spelling, and almost adequate in math. I showed little interest in group work and even less in individual work. I needed to try harder. I would benefit from being held back, again.

Why had I missed work? I'd done everything that was sent to me while I was home, and my plaster and I had ample time to do more. But no, I'd missed work in class; I had fallen behind before I'd broken my leg. I could attribute this to the hours I spent writing and rewriting the exercises until the teacher felt it was time to continue stumbling forwards. It was all a game to the teacher; she was the one who prevented me from keeping up with the class. Her sneaky smile confirmed that she took pride in others' suffering; laughing and joking about the pain she caused, doing it again and again until that person's body and mind gives up.

I refused to repeat Primary Six. I never even discussed it.

I painfully recalled that I'd been forced to try this before in Primary Three. They had presented it like I was given the option of repeating Primary Three, but on reflection it was not my choice. They convinced me that there was a benefit to staying back, but I later realised they had held me back – and worse still, they had done it with my consent. Repeating Primary Three was decided long before it was discussed with me, but they tricked me. They sold the idea of repeating to me as a good thing.

They told me it wasn't my fault. They said that I started school too young. That I was immature. I understood that to mean I was stupid, that I couldn't do the same work as my peers. They said that repeating Primary Three would allow me to grow and mature, and that these things would help with my reading and spelling. I'd get to do the work I had done the past year all over again, and so school would be easier. Would that mean I would recognize it and move from bottom of the class to top? I did very much like that idea.

I could gain a new set of classmates, a fresh start. Maybe I could find some friends? I was going to be moving from being the second youngest to one of the oldest. The oldest kids in my current class were definitely the cleverest and the most popular. Hell yes, I could do with a few friends that were friends all year, not just from three weeks before my birthday and then gone as soon as March rolled in. The photos from my birthday parties are full of smiling children, children from my class, but when the annual class photo was released I was able to name only ten smiles. Mum would be able to name an addition five, which would leave about fifteen blanks where there should be names. But sure enough, next February they would all be my friends again.

I did ask if the girl who was actually younger than me, albeit

Chapter 14

by three days, would have to repeat as well. She was not going to repeat because she was clever, she was popular, she had friends all year round, had beautiful long blonde hair. Why did she not have my mousy hair that was cut the same way as her brothers?

I knew that the fact I was young was not the true reason why I was held back in Primary Three, not that I'd tell the adults I was aware they were lying. That would be impolite. I knew the real reason was that everyone was clever apart from me. Maybe the end of the world would come and save me. It was my new dream – the end of the world. I didn't want world peace, I wanted the opposite.

Little of what they said would happen, happened. In the end, the bits fell apart like an incomplete jigsaw puzzle moved from its supportive backboard.

By doing Primary Three again, my sentence of seven years grew to eight. I did move from being the second youngest to one of the oldest, but what did that matter? Age had nothing to do with my held-back decision. One by one, all the promises that were made fell through within weeks of the new old year. I recognised nothing placed in front of me other than the teacher, the constant fear, the impossible words, and the wish to die. My new friends were gone the second they heard I came from the previous class, not another town. By March I was shattered and all the promises were broken. I couldn't even read what I hadn't been able to read last year.

No, I would not be repeating Primary Six. I did not want to have another year where I was left behind. I wouldn't survive another year with her as my teacher.

From the safety of my bed, I thought about my reading ability. Starting in Primary Three, we had to do our reading in small groups while standing around the teacher's desk. She would ask each person to read aloud, and this was absolutely my most dreaded part of the day. The thought churned in my stomach and my hands grew damp with sweat. I thought I'd throw up or poo myself, or both. I would feel dizzy, so I'd hold my breath and hope I'd faint.

The groups would be divided based on a judgment of our reading ability. I was always in the last group, the one with the poorest readers. I would sit at my desk, supposed to be getting on with another task, but all I could focus on was the group that was currently surrounding the teacher's desk. When would they finish? Which group would she call next? Would it be mine? Did I remember the text? Would she forget to call my group? Would she forget about us daft ones? Would the bell ring and save me?

The bell never rang to save me, and she never forgot. In fact, she took joy in our suffering – the more you struggled, the longer you had to read. She would make you continue until either you got better or she tired of your patheticness and gave up. From the second I started, all I wished for was the end; not the end of reading but the real end, the end that would assure this would never happen again.

Eventually, I gave up on hoping to faint and started pretending to faint, something I got quite good at. You did have to do it correctly, though, and the others who tried it were quite rubbish. Some would throw themselves on the floor like they were diving into a pool, which never fooled the teacher. Others fell but avoided tables and chairs; that was a failed attempt as well. Some even pretended to faint but would end up leaning against the person they were stood beside – as I said, quite rubbish. The key aspect of a good faint was to just forget your legs could hold you up, and all the better if you hit a table or a chair on the way down. Then all you had to do was lie still for a few seconds, and then act a little confused when you came

Chapter 14

round. Easy peasy. All my attempts were successful, and I'd be tucked up in my bed within an hour of "fainting."

We learned about vowels and consonants at school. They were all just letters to me, all of equal importance or non-importance, but I learned the rules. Different letters had different rules. Rules could even change, depending on the neighbouring letter. Some letters were more important than others, and there were five really important ones. Every word had to have at least one of these. This group was even given a special name to reinforce their importance, the "vowels." They did not really like each other as they did not often stand side by side; the other letters were used as a buffer to keep the important but naughty vowels apart. We were told they had different sounds, but I don't think that was a true rule. I often found that they were interchangeable with each other, just so long as every word had at least one.

I wasted hours reading in the evening, and my mother and my father wasted hours with me. They could have been doing other things; *I* could have been doing other things. Mum would read the chapter that was my homework. She would then read it again. Then we would read it together twice. I would then read it to her again and again and again and again and again for as many times as it took until I could read it or at least remember the words in the correct order, whichever came first. Then I had to go and read it to my father. If I stumbled or wavered, I was usually sent back to the dining room to recommence the reading practice. Sometimes he was kind and didn't send me back; sometimes he said I was good, even when I knew I wasn't.

He told me it gets easier, but he never told me when. He would tell me stories of his childhood in Glasgow. He said he didn't have books to read. He didn't even have glasses to drink out off; he drank out of jam jars. Mother said that was rubbish, but how would she know? They never grew up together.

Dad was like me – he did not like school, but he had to go.

After reading to Dad one night, he asked me what I thought of the story, but I had no idea what I'd read. It was just a list of words to me. I knew there was a story hidden in this code, but I was never able to find it. I had a broken connection somewhere. My eyes saw the words, my brain recognised some of the words, and my mouth could even say some of the words, but there was never a story in my head.

My ears were good, though. If someone else spoke the words, my ears would hear them and that would enable my head to do the other half of its role and make a story out of them. But my head couldn't change words into a story by itself. My head had a fault in it. It was my head, so I had a fault.

In any case, the story was not important, only the words that had to be said, the commas for pauses, and the full stops for new breaths. I just had to say the words, so that's what I concentrated on.

I did not tell my father this, though. My reply to his question was one that would not lead onto more questions about the stupid words: "It's okay."

Even with all of this practice, though, when I stood at the teacher's desk the following day and was asked to read, the words on the page looked like I'd never seen them before. I stumbled and stuttered through a few lines, ignoring all of the punctuation, hoping, praying, that it would stop soon. Instead, she would make me keep going. I was never going to get better, but others found entertainment in watching me as my breathing became staggered and uncontrolled. If that went on too long, water would form in my eyes, making the lines of words appear more like the black line on the bottom of the swimming pool.

Chapter 14

My gasping for breath sounded more like those who could not swim and thought they were going to drown when trying so desperately to reach the other side. I never laughed at them for trying to swim; I actually felt a little sorry for them. Swimming was easy. Why did they laugh at me trying to read?

Was that black line in the swimming pool made up of words too? I'd always thought it was a solid black line.

If the build-up of water in my eyes continued, they would overflow and run down my cheeks, raising the amusement levels within my fellow readers and watchers to comedy status. Only my cool, wet skin stood in place during reading; the rest of me all fell down into my legs. I was a thawing snowman, soon to become an unidentifiable blob on the floor. People would have to guess that I was once a person.

At some point the teacher would ask me to stop and an icy cold sense of relief would run through me, as if refilling my melted insides. Unlike the broken snowman, I could begin to take form again. My breathing would become controlled and natural again, and I could feel my body climbing out of my legs and refilling my chest and my arms and my hands and my head. I'd get my feeling back into my fingers and reclaim whatever control I had of my broken brain, and I'd know I'd survived another reading task until the new sudden thaw of tomorrow.

There would be the scolding, of course; the accusation of not doing the required homework the night before, when in truth it was all I had done the night before. I seldom had time to go out and play with my brothers as my homework took most, if not all, of the evening. I'd always take too long doing my homework, but at least after homework came bedtime, that peaceful time when no one could hurt me or make me feel foolish.

On occasion, I would try and explain to the teacher that in fact I had spent many hours reading the stupid chapter with my parents, but that only resulted in her saying I was lying. No one could be as bad as I was at reading if they had done their homework. If I continued lying, it would result in a trip to see the headmaster.

There was no point arguing with her. I was bad at reading, even though I'd read the chapter many times the night before. It was far quicker and easier to admit that I had not done my homework and agree when she stated I was the person in most need of doing my homework every single night. I'd agree to anything if it meant I could return to my chair and be ignored for a few minutes. It was a lie, but it was the correct answer as far as the teacher was concerned. Teachers liked to be correct.

Lying became quite easy, often times easier than explaining the truth. It was hard for me to believe that after hours of reading with my parents, I still could not read the same words the next day. How could I then expect her to believe me when I claimed I'd done my homework?

I was lazy in my written English as well as my reading; I was told of my laziness with enough frequency that I knew it to be true. They told me to try harder, and I did, but every extra effort to spell correctly was met with a comment about the "lack of effort or care in my work."

I liked the idea of math, of numbers rather than words. My brother was doing well in maths, very well, and it gave me hope that I too would do well. Maths is not about whether or not you get the correct answer, it's about the path you take to work it out. Finally, a subject that the answer was not right or wrong, pass or fail, but one that could thank you for trying.

Escaping was all I could think of, all that I dreamed of; the idea obsessed my every waking moment. It was the last thing

Chapter 14

I thought of before sleeping and the first thing I thought of upon waking. I imagined myself free of school, free of reading, free of homework, free of my broken brain. I imagined myself free of life.

15

Even though I was told I was behind in my schooling, I was certain that I would not be repeating Primary Six. I had absolutely no intention of doing a nine-year sentence in this hellhole which was meant to be the best years of my life. I felt like a plaything to be kicked around and abused in front of the class or school as my teacher wished.

I knew my Primary Six teacher was the wickedest of all the teachers so far. She had decided to take a dislike to my handwriting. She would claim that it was unreadable and send me back to rewrite whatever I had just completed. This was a time-consuming task, although an easy enough one to complete. Occasionally, I would attempt to write even messier in the hope that I would be sent back to rewrite it more clearly. The class and I were used to this humiliation; it was an old one, and luckily one that did not produce new openings to make fun of me.

One day I stood in the dreaded teacher's desk queue waiting for the inevitable bollocking, looking forward to returning to my seat to rewrite as the others moved onto the next task. She must have noticed that rewriting did not bother me, though, so she caught me off guard as she called the class attention.

Chapter 15

"Now class, put down your pencils. Rhona has written this three times today, and I still can't read it because her handwriting is so bad. I doubt she can even read it. Rhona, please read your work to the class."

I'd do anything other than this – absolutely, unconditionally anything. I looked at her, fear oozing out of my every pore. She smiled that putrid, disconcerting, sneaky smile that she had truly mastered. She knew she had beaten me. She knew I hated this. Crafty bitch. I was thinking about launching a physical attack. If I'd brought my pencil, I could have rammed it in her eye or neck, or even my own eye or neck; if it had hurt in a bottom cheek, it must hurt more in an eye. It might even kill her if I was lucky.

I knew I was capable of murder. After all, I'd murdered my brother's hamster, Hammy, a few years before. Officially it would have been "accidental hamster-slaughter," but I had no official defence lawyer on my side and my own defence was inadequate. The judge and jury of my family tried me for murder, and I was unanimously found guilty.

It happened on a summer evening when Evan was out. Hammy got up early and was licking the ball-bearing at the end of his drinking bottle. Mum was in the kitchen. I asked her if I could take the little creature out of his cage and lock him in his ball so he could crash into walls and doors and heaters, occasionally getting wedged and requiring rescuing. My brother and I used to watch him for hours, always ready to help when he got stuck. She said no. So instead, I watched him for a while; he ate some of his food and then just sat still.

Father was watching TV. I asked him if I could take the hamster out and he said, "Ask your mother." That was pointless, since she never changed her mind.

I went back to the cage and decided to bring him out

anyway. I opened the hatch and stretched my arm in, gently scooping up the little furry creature and hoisting him towards his impending freedom. As I was pulling him out, the door snapped closed and my hand and its contents got caught. I got a fright, and so did Hammy. It all happened so fast that I don't know the order of things, and that fact went against me in the trial for his murder.

The things that happened in those few seconds were: the door of his cage snapped closed, I dropped Hammy, and Hammy bit me. Hammy looked okay after; he was sort of walking about. My hand was bleeding though, so I had to act fast. I opened the door again and then lifted the roof of his little red house which acted as his bed. I moved him in there, wished him a heartfelt speedy recovery, and replaced the roof. I then went to my room, collecting a towel from the bathroom to wrap my hand en route.

Minutes passed, quite a few. I prayed for Hammy to recover and my hand to stop bleeding. I was just beginning to think everything might be okay when I heard my mother.

"Rhona…Come…Here…Right…Now." I instantly knew I was in trouble; so did my stomach, as it fell into my legs. I reported to Mother as demanded. She was stood by the cage, along with my dad. Hammy was in the corner of his cage, motionless. I had crushed him.

My first line of defence was to deny everything. I claimed I'd not touched the hamster as she had denied my request to put him in his ball.

Then they saw my hand.

They linked the blood visible on the sawdust to me and not the hamster, and this is where things really turned bad for me. I had well and truly lost this round. I'd attempted to get the hamster out of his cage after being told not to do so, then lied

Chapter 15

about it when asked – my mother did not know which of those two things were worse. I'd also got bitten and attempted to hide both the injury and the hamster. I had genuinely thought he might be okay, but my voice was not heard through my tears. The fact that I'd hid him in his bed indicated to my parents that I knew he was close to death. He had crawled out of his bed and died in full view of all.

Hammy was not even my hamster. What would I say to his owner when he returned? How would I explain myself? There were so many questions, and there was no time to answer then. I'd killed the hamster by accident, but the result was the same. It really was my fault; if only I'd listened to my mother, then Hammy would be fine. But no, I tried to take him out anyway, and now he was dead.

I was sent to my room to think about what I'd done, but all I could think about was the dead hamster. If only the little thing had stayed in his house bed, they would have thought he had been lucky enough to die in his sleep and I'd have thought of something to say about my hand. But it was not to be, and now I was a murderer.

I felt very sorry that I'd murdered Hammy. Everyone treated me like it was not an accident, that I had somehow intended to kill him. They never understood me. Would they ever?

I would never be sorry that I had murdered this teacher, though, not even when I was in prison. I was already in prison, but I was not armed with a pencil. She asked again in her slow, angry/excited voice for me to start reading my work to the class. I wanted to quit this game; it had not been fun for a very long time. I promised myself that tonight was the night. Tonight, I'd eat the crystals.

"Please read your work to the class!" she bellowed, as if I was deaf as well as stupid.

I started slowly concentrating on each word, one at a time, but my eyes would jump to the next word before they had finished looking at the one my mouth was currently expected to be pronouncing. Other words from other lines were jumping for my attention. The words kept moving, changing size and boldness, every one of them demanding my respect and an immediate response. There were no breathing points, no commas for pauses or full stops for breaths. This was not my work. These were not my words. I would not have used these words. I'd never seen these words before. This could not be my writing, even though it was in my book. My words rolled into one long, incomprehensible noise with no connection to the syllable that came before it.

I was actually dying. I couldn't breathe, I couldn't see, I couldn't think.

"Enough!" she called, seconds before I died.

Oh thank god, I thought.

"Enough. So, I think it's clear to everyone that you cannot read your own handwriting, and if I could it would be littered with mistakes."

My eyes were broken again and were overflowing, and my nose was rapidly reaching maximum capacity.

"That's right, cry like a baby."

She did not need to tell me, I was already doing it.

"I tell you what, let's go and get you some plasticine to play with. Everyone, back to work. Rhona and I are going to get some plasticine from Primary One."

We walk across the filled gym hall, and I felt a thousand eyes piercing my soul. I could almost breathe again, but my skin was cold and wet all over.

She stopped outside the door. "Do you wish to knock or should I?" she asked.

Chapter 15

"I don't want their plasticine," I explained in the most controlled voice I could muster.

"Why not?" she inquired.

"Many reasons!"

"Give me one," she insisted.

"I'm not a baby," I said, trying very hard not to cry like one.

She turned from the door and walked slowly back towards her class. I followed behind like she was the queen.

She muttered, as my mother had told me many times, "Rhona, you really are very special." I think she said it more to herself than to me.

When she opened the classroom door all eyes turned to us, and she bellowed, "Do your own work, everyone!"

I returned to my desk and commenced rewriting the words that seemed so alien a few minutes earlier, but now looked so familiar. I felt utterly drained, like my life had been sucked from me. I was sure my heart would slow and stop and nobody would notice while I was busy rewriting. The end must be close – I was so very tired.

I was hopeless at reading. I was just utterly hopeless. Every time I heard "Rhona," I thought "oh god no," wondered "why, oh why?" Everyone knew that I was hopeless, going to get nowhere, going to amount to nothing. How would I ever get a job when I could not even read properly? I wasn't clever, wasn't good looking, wasn't even popular. How long could I struggle on like this? What was the point of struggling on?

Why the punishment? Is it for some greater good? Was I rubbish at everything so that all the others could feel better about themselves? Did my misery make them feel better? Did my loneliness and pain lessen their own? When would my prayers be answered? When was my last breath? When would they let me be? When would they forget about me? When would they leave me alone and let me be happy in my own thoughts? I bargained with God. If he'd make this stop, make them stop forcing me to read, I'd be good forever. He never helped.

If I repeated Primary Six, I would be stuck with this hellish teacher for another year. If I repeated Primary Six, I would be stuck in this hellish prison for another year. I refused. I simply said no. I would not to do it. No, No, No, no, no, no, No, No, NO!

"You can't make me."

"I'll run away."

"You don't love me."

"I hate you."

I knew these were likely very hurtful words for my parents to hear from their child. I knew they believed they were doing the right thing – the thing the school told them was best – but these were the sentences I used to explain I would not be repeating Primary Six. It was the first time that I'd openly told my parents some of my thoughts. This upset them; I made Mum cry and was sent to my room. I held "I want to die" and "I'll kill myself" in reserve for a dire emergency. I made my own personal guarantee that I would not be held back in Primary Six, but it was best that I did not share my thoughts with them in future. That way they would not get upset. Mum would not cry.

In the end, it was decided that I would be permitted to continue through Primary Six and on to Primary Seven if I went back to school and kept up with the class. Otherwise, I'd have to repeat Primary Six again; or, I would have to complete my plan to ensure I'd not be able to repeat Primary Six, no matter what.

16

Nice is possibly one of my favourite words. Nice was beautiful. Nice was pleasant. Nice was polite. Nice was even gracious and respectful. Nice I could spell; nice would not get the loathed red pen. I used nice a lot. Good was excellent, it was exceptional and superior. My teachers were cruel, ghastly, faulty human beings; they were simply bad bad bad. They made me miserable and distressed for most of the best years of my life. They made me sad, very sad. My Primary Six teacher was the worst of them all, but I had previously learned that many of my teachers were out to get me.

By Primary Four, I had ended up in the support classroom – the retard class. The retards had to be segregated from the clever kids in case the dumbness was contagious like the common cold. Common sense was a thing, so common stupidity must also be a thing. However, no one really talked to me about this group as it was my group, and no one ever tells you the real truth when it's your group.

The retard class was quite a safe place for a while. We had a male teacher who was kind and never shouted at me, and I felt cleverer than some of the other people in there. In fact, I felt that if we were sat in tables of cleverness, I may not be at the last one. But, as everything worked against me, we did not sit in tables of cleverness.

They said I spoke well – spoke a different vocabulary than the one I wrote. My teachers said this was because I was lazy. I hated seeing the red pen, a far-too-regular unwelcome visitor on my work. I aimed for a piece of work to be returned with no red pen; I dreamed of it being returned with a star sticker. I did not want a gold star, I knew I'd never get a gold star, but if I got a blue one, an effort star, I'd be so pleased that all I had to do was try harder.

The retard class teacher was shouting at the smelly kid one day. I don't know why, maybe because he had not washed his hair or hands. All I knew was when a teacher is shouting at someone, you don't want to be the next person they talk to. I never looked or laughed as someone else was getting yelled at – I was quietly grateful it was not me, and I hoped I was not going to be next. But this teacher did turn and start talking to me, and even though he had been yelling seconds earlier, his voice changed faster than a click of your fingers. That was new. I'd never seen any teacher do that before, and I was full of admiration. There was a chance, a very slim chance, a glimmer of hope, that I may not get shouted at unless I did something to deserve shouting.

At first I did not like going to the special classroom, the retard class. Everyone saw me leaving the regular classroom and they all knew I was going to join the other stupid people. However, it had to be a plus for all of us that I was leaving. I would get a rest from them, and I would not hold up their progress or stunt their development. When I returned, they were interested to know what I had done, not that I told them. They would have been disappointed to know that I actually did very similar work in there as they had done in my absence.

Chapter 16

The only difference was the teacher sat beside you and did not shout.

We read a lot in the retard class. He gave me a bit of cardboard with a hole cut in it so you could see only one line at a time. Once you read that line you moved it along and read the next, fairly easy stuff. I knew and recognised most of the words, so it was a straightforward task so long as I stopped and breathed at the dots – later to be named full stops – and did not panic that the next word was going to be unreadable. If it was, he would read it and I'd move the card along and continue to read words. At the end of reading one day he asked me what I thought was going to happen next in the story. I explained that there would be more words – probably no pictures, just words – and when the words finished, someone would give me another book of words, and this would likely continue until at least the end of primary school.

It was in this class that I learned about trick letters. I somehow always knew my name had a trick letter; I frequently had to remind people of the "h." One day, this teacher asked me how to spell my name. *Aha*, I thought, he knew of my trick letter but was unsure where it was. I spelt out my R.H.O.N.A with confidence and pride, only to be asked to spell my surname. But there were no trick letters in my surname, so why was he asking? Was he making a fool out of me? I refused to fall into the trap. I simply said, "It's spelt like it sounds," something that had been said to me again and again and again. I know this helps other people spell, but it never helped me. I never really understood the saying. He did, though, and replied "Of course, how silly of me!"

This conversation was never spoken of again, but something deep in my stomach told me that it had not gone as well as I thought, and that extreme caution should be used in this class in case there were more tricks coming.

In Primary Five, I came up with a trick of my own. The teacher gave us an exercise, and I took care to use only words that I knew how to spell. As a result, my work was returned with no red corrections for the first time. I was pretty pleased with myself, but the teacher did not share my sense of achievement. I reassured myself that I had done well, that I had returned a bit of work with no spelling corrections. I deserved a star, maybe even a gold star.

My parents were called to the school that day, although I did not know why. Is this not what they wanted? I reminded them that there was no red pen in the entire exercise. They did not argue the point, but now they wanted me to write the words I couldn't spell, and not to worry about the red pen. *What the hell's the point of that*, I thought. First they want no red pen, now they want all red pen. They change the rules as soon as I've learned them. I hated their grown-up games. They pretended to want to help me, but they were the ones who could not decide what they wanted.

They had stopped talking; they were all looking at me, searching for an impossible answer. I said okay and they seemed pleased with themselves, but I had missed the question! They wanted me to write the words I couldn't spell? Or write the words I said? Why? I saved myself from voicing that question. Okay, I would keep the red pen out of my work. Okay, I was going to have to make some mistakes and allow the red pen an appearance, but I would decide which words it would attack. Okay, I would change the way I talk. Okay, I'd use baby language if that was what they wanted. Okay. Okay. Okay.

I would have to remind myself that "the rules have just changed and you have to keep up, Rhona." The red pen was no friend of mine.

Chapter 16

Today was a success, no matter what they said. I knew that I had done well, and I didn't need a blue star to prove it. Having no red pen on my work deserved a gold star, but the rules had just changed. I would decide where and how often the red pen visited my work, I assured my inner soul. The ever-changing minds of grown-ups were hard to handle and even harder to keep up with.

My new plan ended up being entirely ineffective. When I stuck to using mostly words I could spell and the occasional one that I couldn't, I got told off. When I used more words that I couldn't spell, I got told off for that too. I liked using words I could spell more – I liked avoiding the red pen – but it took too long to think of a sentence that only used words I could spell, and I would fall too far behind in class.

The rules had changed, and I could no longer win the game.

17

When it was time to return to Primary Six, I went back to school in a full-length plaster and crutches. Father dropped me off every morning and carried my bag to the class or the gate, where a "friend" would offer to collect and carry it for me. Amazingly, they did so.

The first week my leg throbbed and my toes had gotten fat by the time Father collected me at 3:00 p.m. The teacher ignored me and I moved on to new activities with the rest of the class, whether my last activity was marked or not. My neighbour took my work for correction, so there was no yelling and little rewriting. It was easy to keep up. I did not have to navigate around trick questions.

The other students were very interested in my crutches and they all wanted to give them a test drive, but I was reluctant to part with them. I feared they would not be returned, and I really did depend on their strength and power. However, I finally had something that someone else wanted, and it got harder and harder to say no.

To share was to risk that the wooden supports would not be returned, but to share could also mean having friends. I refused at first, frightened of the consequences, but the more I refused

Chapter 17

the more they pleaded and bargained and the higher my fear climbed that the wooden supports would not be returned.

My wanting of friends and their wanting of wooden supports eventually wore me down. I handed them over one break-time on the promise they would be returned to me. The children changed the height to suit themselves and, as I had feared, when the bell summoned us back to the torture chambers my friends abandoned my wooden support legs on the other side of the hall, which was rapidly emptying. I was going to be late, and I was going to be in trouble when instead I desperately needed gold stars. Somebody was going to demand I be held back. I would have to kill myself, and I couldn't trust the Do Not Eat packet of crystals to do the job.

I'd once again trusted someone who had tricked me. I did not need anyone to ask me the question I already know was coming: "When will you learn, Rhona, you silly girl?" Sadly, I did not know the answer.

An older woman passed – I don't think I'd seen her before. "Do you need some help?" she asked gently.

Was that not obvious? I was on the opposite side of the hall to my crutches and had a plaster that felt longer than my leg and heavier than myself, but I recalled my training. Do not say the first thing that comes into your head.

"Yes, my crutches are over there, could you please get them for me?" I replied, slightly panicked.

"Yes I can," she said as she walked across the hall, collected them, and returned.

I went to work unscrewing the bolts.

"What are you doing, Rhona?" she enquired.

"They changed the height; I need to put them back." I answered abruptly.

"I see."

"And now I'm going to be late to class and get in trouble, and as usual it's not my fault but I'll get the blame. They are going to try and make me repeat Primary Six again," I muttered as I busily worked on the bolts, forgetting my training.

"Whose fault is it, Rhona?"

"Those who stole my crutches."

"Did they really steal them, or did you give them?"

"I gave them for a borrow, isn't it obvious I need them? They did not return them, that's stealing." I was angry now.

"I suppose so." Her voice remained gentle despite my harsh tones.

"And now I'll get in trouble the second I open that door," I said steadying myself, nodding at the door.

"Let me get the door for you, Rhona." She trotted behind me as I moved quite swiftly on my stabilizing wooden legs.

"Okay. Thank you," I said, her kindness finally registering with me.

She opened the door and I hopped through, feeling all eyes drilling into me, trying to prepare myself for the inevitable. My eyes were already blinking too quickly.

"Please excuse Rhona's slight lateness, there was a small issue with her crutches that will be addressed in time," she announced to the class.

"That's no problem at all, are you okay Rhona?" the teacher said, rushing towards me as if there were a fire behind her. She looked like the same witch as before, moved the same way, but those words she was using – who did they belong to?

I stared in a mix of astonishment and bewilderment, feeling eternal gratitude towards this woman, this teacher who must have just taught clever children as I'd never been taught by her. I liked her, she had helped me. I stepped back from the fire-driven teacher in case she was not going to stop before hitting us both.

Chapter 17

"I'm fine." *Just gullible*, I thought, but had the sense not to announce the second part, remembering my training once again. I didn't need to make the announcement; they were already fully aware of my gullibility. I hopped across the room to take my seat.

This wasn't the first time I had been tricked by a classmate. One day, when I was in Primary Five, I was offered a trade: to let a girl beat me in the qualifying race for the swimming gala in return for her friendship. It was a race that I fully expected to win. Swimming was something I was good at, something I actually enjoyed. It also provided me with some peace and quiet; once my ears filled with water, the world around me disappeared. I enjoyed swimming, but I saw no importance in it. Swimming was something you did to relax, to fill time. To waste time. Being good at swimming wouldn't get me a job – you had to be good at school to do that.

So, I took the girl up on the offer. After all, what was one qualifying race? There had been hundreds of races, and there would soon be more at the gala the next week. I wanted a friend, a best friend, so that the grown-ups would stop talking about how I was not mixing with others. The back crawl heat came and went, and I was second – a mark of failure – but now I had a best friend. I was pleased with my effort, although my swimming teacher made it perfectly clear she was not. She advised me to stop daydreaming and start concentrating, saying that if I went any slower I'd be at risk of drowning. She did not understand the sacrifice I'd made: one poxy race for a new best friend. I'd done the better thing.

The next day, the entire world knew I'd lost the back crawl qualifier, and that same world predicted I would lose the swimming gala as well. I ignored them and went in search of my new best friend, but she was very busy with her other best friends. I was relayed messages through her runners that all I needed to do now was more of the same in the competition. I sat alone between the coats, pretending not to hear their taunts, and cursed myself for giving up the only thing I was good at. I'd been tricked. I told them so, but the messages were relayed back that I had misunderstood the deal. I had to lose the gala to gain the best friend.

    I could think of many examples of my gullibility. But after the theft of the wooden legs, I assured myself that was the end. I was going to grow up and stand up for myself.

18

On my return to Primary Six with my broken tibia the teacher mostly stopped hassling me, especially after the day that I fell – the day that my teacher became frightened of my father.

That day, I was hopping over to her desk with some work to be marked when I tripped. I'd actually being trying to hop over a school bag, which was my new trick, and since I no longer lent anyone else my crutches it was a unique one. Anyway, as I hopped the owner of the bag leaned over to reach into it and caught my plastered leg, and down I went.

I quickly realized my plaster was cracked. Everyone rushed about. They asked me if my leg hurt; I got the indication that the correct answer was yes, so that was the answer I gave.

I was still trying to understand correct answers. I knew the correct answer was not always the truth, but it was equally important to tell the truth all the time. There were strict conditions about what to say when, and I only knew some of them.

For example, Evan had been sick a few weeks prior – he was coughing and coughing and coughing. The doctor had prescribed medication that Evan had to take twice a day, a syrup that was meant to be strawberry flavoured. Evan did not like it, and he screamed when mother tried to give it to him. They explained how it would make him better and ease his throat, but Evan kept his lips sealed as if it was poisonous. Dad had some, and so did Mum, and so did I, thus proving that it was safe. Dad even made yum noises and asked for more, yet Evan was not to be fooled. He had decided he was not having any of it, so his lips remained sealed.

Evan's cough never got better. He had to go back to the doctor, and as it was before I started school I went with him. The doctor looked in his throat and confirmed it was no better. He asked Mother if he had taken the syrup twice a day and she confirmed he had, producing the empty bottle. She must have been confused, so I reminded her that Evan had actually screamed when she tried to give it to him, and she had poured it down the kitchen sink when Evan still refused to have any. The doctor said that he didn't blame Evan, that it was horrible stuff, and prescribed tablets.

We had just got through the front door when Mother became very cross with me. She informed me that I shouldn't have said that Evan would not take the medication or that she poured it down the drain. I should not have told the truth. The truth in this instance was definitely not the correct answer.

Another example is that when I was shopping with Mum and strangers asked if I liked my brothers, I had to say yes. I had said no once, which was the truth, but that was not the correct answer. And later, when I was older and they asked if I liked school, I had to say yes, although that was definitely not the truthful answer.

I learned to distance the truth from the responses I gave. The correct answer was the answer the questioner wanted or expected, the one that did not lead to sorrowful looks between the adults or being told off once you entered the safety of home.

Chapter 18

The correct answers were often a lie, but as lies were bad to tell I had to pretend the correct answer, that is the lie, was the truth. It was very hard to remember what I had to say as the correct answer instead of what I knew to be the truth, especially if the question was repeated later. I could get myself in trouble for lying if I gave a different answer even if both answers were lies, including the one that was supposed to be correct. You can't say the truth to people who ask me about my brothers or school. You especially can't say the truth to doctors.

So, my leg with its broken plaster: did it hurt? In truth, it did not hurt more or less than any other time. But they were satisfied with my correct answer of "yes."

My parents were called and my father turned up. He asked me what had happened. I simply said I was taking my work up to be marked and tripped. It was the truth – maybe not the entire truth, but true nonetheless. He then spoke to the witch and asked if this was true, to which she agreed. There was no point lying as the entire class had witnessed the event.

He enquired why I, with a broken leg, had to take work up to her, who did not have a broken leg. But he did not wait for her answer. He asked how long I'd been doing this for. Again, no time for her to answer. I could tell he was cross, really cross. He wasn't even shouting, that's how cross he was. But strangely, he was not cross with me for falling, he was cross with her. I wasn't sure why. She had actually been almost nice to me since I'd returned to her class. She'd stopped picking on me, although I knew it was only a matter of time before she would start again. But why was Dad so angry at her? He must have been annoyed that he had to close the garage to come and get me. I was lucky he was not angry at me.

He said some odd things, things that everyone knew. That she was the adult and was responsible for the children in her care. He said he was dumbfounded at her behaviour. There was time now for her to answer, but she said nothing. I was going to have to find out what dumbfounded meant.

Complete with wooden supports, I hopped out to the car, which was oddly parked in the No Parking section right at the school gate. Dad asked if my leg was sore and I had to say yes, a little. I couldn't change my story as they would know that I'd lied before. We picked up Mum from the house and headed back to Inverness.

When we arrived, it was like they knew I was coming. The x-ray was ready. The non-white-coat-wearing man asked me to smile – ha, no way, you're not going to trick me twice. I might be stupid but I'm not a fool!

The bone was still straight so they did not have to realign it. I was pleased I would not have to deal with the nurse with all the daft questions again; after all, I had no update on my previous replies. I was whisked into the plaster room next. It looked so different to the last time and was a lot quieter, but I supposed more people ski on a Saturday than on a Tuesday. I was allowed to go home the same day, and it wasn't long before I was back in bed with my fresh, heavy plaster.

It had been an interesting morning, strange even, and as I tried to understand it I drifted off to sleep to the comfort and freedom of my dreams.

The best part of this whole ordeal was that I was allowed to stay home for a while, out of the awful teacher's reach. I knew she'd be really horrible to me as Dad had been so very cross with her, so I was happy to stay away from her as long as possible.

I was back in class by the end of the following week – my choice. Mum would have permitted me to stay at home longer, but I was still very frightened of the "need to repeat." Nobody

Chapter 18

had mentioned that to me in a while, but that did not mean that they were not plotting behind my back.

Primary Six was not horrible on my return, and the teacher did not take my father's anger out on me. In fact, she ignored me completely. It was bliss. It was so much easier to keep up with the work without the dread of being picked on and forbidden to move on to the next task. I did what I could and copied my neighbour's work whenever possible.

Perhaps I would survive this year after all.

19

A few days after my return to Primary Six, the teacher announced that the tables and seats were to be rearranged. I was told to sit in the corner, out of the way and out of danger.

I wondered why teachers insisted on moving the class around. There was always the risk of being placed at the stupid table if they decided to sit us in order of intelligence. I didn't like sitting at the stupid table; there, copying your neighbour's work was next to useless.

There was something about us stupid kids. I never thought I smelt bad or excessively scratched myself, but the other stupid kids did. They all scratched themselves like they had nits or fleas or both. Some of them scratched until their skin bled and then scratched some more – I supposed it was their attempt at escaping the table, the class, their lives. I did not scratch, but I always felt dirty at that table.

This time, the new table arrangement was alphabetically in twos. This was good news. The girl whose name was closest to mine was clever and nice – she felt sorry for me and would help me when the teacher wasn't looking. I wondered if she would be disappointed with the seating rearrangements.

My new neighbour hated swimming. She was always so

Chapter 19

very frightened that she would die, that it was just a matter of time until she sank to the bottom. I tried to keep an eye on her while we swam. I frequently swam beside her, trying to be encouraging, trying to show that it would be okay. Trying to repay the kindness she showed me in class.

During one class, when we were writing a story, my no-swimmer neighbour was sneakily proofreading my work and writing incorrectly spelt words on the side of her paper for me to copy. She wrote "goddess" and pointed to where I should insert it into my story, which I did.

As I stood at the teacher's desk, waiting for my work to be marked, Miss Primary Six picked that one word and asked me to read the sentence that contained it. I couldn't read it. I didn't know the word my non-swimmer neighbour had given me, and I couldn't read.

She screamed and screamed and screamed about cheating, about spelling, about reading, spitting all over me in the process. I had to concentrate on just standing and breathing. I had no energy for listening or answering; all I could do was try to stand and breathe. It felt like years, but when I eventually got back to my seat my non-swimmer neighbour was crying softly.

My neighbour used to talk about getting in trouble at home when her parents would catch her reading at night once she was meant to be asleep. They would catch her by seeing her light on under her door, but she had found a way around this. She found a torch, and after she was meant to be asleep she would hide under the cover and read by torch light.

Why did she like reading so much? What was she reading that could possibly be better than dreams?

Would I prefer to read or swim? Reading would be far more useful in keeping the adults quiet about my progress, but I liked swimming. As I thought hard about the choice, I realised that I did not have a choice. I could swim, so I couldn't read. There was no point in wasting time thinking about a choice that was not even mine to make.

Besides, Mum read to me at bedtime anyway, setting me up to dream of raising a lion cub called Elsa. *Born Free* was my favourite book. It had been read many times, but I'd never looked at a single word. I also liked the book *The Witches*. It was real, too; I knew my teachers were all witches. They hated children, especially me. They hated our smell. Even I did not like how some of the kids smelt. But I did not want to cause the other kids harm, not like the witch teachers. If only I could live a short life and kill all the witches at a conference.

The teacher eventually rearranged the seating plan, and I was yet again at the stupid table. My ex-neighbour was at the clever table, unable to offer me any more kindnesses.

20

My plaster was shortened with each visit to Inverness, and then one day it was cut the full length of its side.

The doctor insisted that I see and hear the plaster cutting device before he started. It looked like an electric pizza cutter. He reassured me that it made a lot of noise but did not cut skin. He wanted to show me by putting it on my arm before starting on the plaster on my leg. He was very insistent about the demonstration, although I was not sure why. If he said it would not cut skin, I believed him. Surely it would not be a trick. But, I was trying to be less gullible, and I had realised that this sort of thing was a warning sign I usually missed. What someone says/claims/states is actually the opposite of what happens. Now I was worried this electric pizza cutter would cut my leg.

I agreed to the demonstration on my arm and watched as the cutter screamed into life and approached my forearm. The second it made contact with its target, the blade stopped. My mother had said once that I could break something by just looking at it, but I never believed her until now, looking at the electric pizza cutter motionless on my forearm.

He lifted it off my arm and the thing buzzed back into action.

He then touched my arm again and it broke again. It reminded me of our Operation board game, with the little organs that you had to get out with tweezers without touching the side of the hole and starting the buzzing noise that would persist until the tweezers stopped touching the side.

The pizza cutter ran slowly down both sides of the plaster and then it was time for the unveiling. They lifted the top half off to reveal my leg, but it wasn't my leg – it was a very thin white leg with big ugly bits of skin flaking off. This leg that we were all looking at felt unattached and looked unmatched to its partner. The two rulers that I'd lost down the plaster were relocated. Moisturiser cream was rubbed into the pale skin; it was cold, biting cold. They held my leg up and slipped the cradle of the other half of the plaster out. My leg really did look odd.

The specialist came and declared a pass, and I was to be re-plastered with a below-the-knee walking plaster. The process seemed simple again, with the three layers of bandaging; the last one had to be soaked before unrolling.

Walking was a little odd, almost like walking with one ski boot on, but it was doable. I was much faster on my wooden legs though.

On the journey back home, I wondered why the first plaster had taken so long to set and made me stay overnight in the hospital when the other two did not. Maybe they had tricked me. Maybe my parents had been late that afternoon. Maybe they knew that the doctors could not plaster my broken leg without them being there. Maybe they knew that plaster takes time to set, and that if they did not turn up they would have to keep me in the hospital. Maybe they just wanted to be rid of me for a while. Maybe they just need a break from me.

I needed to gain control over my wandering thoughts. I told myself that my parents loved me very much and they had not

Chapter 20

been late to the hospital, either initially or to collect me the following day, even though they *had* been late!

Now that I was walking crutch-free, I was back to walking up to the teacher's desk, back to walking into the danger zone. Mum told me if I got tired of standing that I should just walk back to my seat, and if the teacher said anything to tell her that my leg was heavy and I needed to sit down. She said not to suffer like I had with my accident in Primary One.

I logged the advice. Standing was easy, I could just put weight on my not-so-broken leg, but Mum and Dad had never broken anything so they weren't to know. If the teacher started on me I'd just walk away, and when she started screaming "Don't walk away from me when I'm talking to you!" I'd look over my shoulder and explain that my plaster was heavy and that I needed to sit down. I had a plan to keep myself safe from her.

I repeated my plan in my head while waiting each and every time at her desk. I knew I had a tendency to get panicked and forget things once she started shouting at me. My mother had given me a plan, but I needed to remember it.

If she was really bad to me, I could faint-fall and Dad would come and he'd be dumbfounded again. I had two safety plans, and I was almost at the end of year.

21

One day, like magic, my leg was not broken anymore and I parted company with my best friend, the life-saving plaster. When I was reunited with my leg again, it was almost unrecognizable – it was certainly detached, despite all the muscle and blood vessels physically demonstrating its attached status.

I was like the opposite of an amputee. An amputee has pain in a phantom leg; my leg was back but felt gone. It was as if my brain had taught itself to abandon the leg that had not done anything in weeks. It had discarded the limb as useless and worthless. It had figured out how to function without the leg, and so the leg was cut out of life's necessities. I could learn to do this with people who did nothing positive for me: make my brain cut them out of my necessity of life. I could abandon them and figure out how to function without them. I formalised my list of names:
1. Teachers.
2. X-ray man.
3. Dentists.
4. Former friendly girl.
5. Black Labrador at the end of the road.

Chapter 21

I knew my leg was useless. The doctors said that my leg was in fact back, whether my brain liked it or not, and it was clear I was wasting their time by not using it. I tried to tell them that it was broken, that I couldn't stand on it, but it was no use.

The specialist was cross at me, I guessed because I would not stand on it and I had to stand on it to prove that it was no longer broken, even though it was. Mum was silent, but I knew she was cross at me too. I didn't like people being cross at me. I didn't want to waste the specialist's time, but I knew I'd fall down if I stood on the leg.

I made an attempt to stand on my broken leg, even though I knew I would fail. I stood on it for a millisecond and got my other foot on the floor before gravity took over, and the specialist sent Mum and me on our way. He was like my teachers, having no time to spend on someone who did not want to try, did not want to help herself. His assistant was less harsh. He permitted me to take my wooden supports home and said I would see him in the clinic in a few weeks, by which time he reassured me I'd have confidence in the leg and would not need the crutches. This fellow was all about the reassurance.

I'd have to learn to walk again, although I did not remember learning the first time. Why did I always forget the important things? I did have an advantage now compared to when I first learned – one of my legs and feet knew what to do, so I was halfway there already.

Day one of my return to life plaster-less I spent in bed doing my dancing exercises to see if I could get my leg muscles working again.

Years ago, when I was four or so, Mother had seen an advert in the local paper stating that a new class of highland dancers was due to start. She asked if I'd like to go. I had no idea what it was, but if it meant going somewhere I was in. I started the following Tuesday night. The class was pretty straightforward; all you had to do was copy what the person at the front was doing. I went the Tuesday after that and the Tuesday after that.

They said highland dancing was good for me. They said it gave me confidence. They said I was good at it. To me, it was simply copying work, and not the type of copying that you had to hide. Then, once you'd copied it a few times, the teacher expected you to remember what you'd done. I don't know how the others seemed to forget. They had just been copying the steps moments before. Most of it was in sets of four, and everyone could count to four. Even I could count to four.

As I got older, we spent most Saturdays at dancing competitions. It turned out I was quite good at remembering how to count to four and what my feet should be doing. On these Saturdays, I could be a winner. We competed in ages and I never knew any of my fellow competitors in my group, so I didn't have to be stupid on Saturdays. Instead, I won trophies and cups on these Saturdays.

Come Monday, though, I was not allowed to take my trophy or cup to school. I was not allowed to show that I was good at something. Some other girls, younger than me, were allowed to take *their* dancing trophies to school, and they went round all the classrooms showing off their prizes, parading them like they were better than me. My classmates were sure that I had either lost to these younger girls or had not won anything as I had no proof to back up my weekend success story. The mothers of these younger girls even organised a show to demonstrate their talent, and I had to sit in the audience beside my classmates, who were now even more certain that I couldn't even dance. I could see the mistakes the two made, but everyone else was oblivious to them. It was humiliating and belittling, and I wanted to be free from it all.

Chapter 21

I wanted to get back to dancing now that my plaster was off, but my leg was weak. It felt broken, not healed. They said swimming would strengthen the muscles again, so I headed back to swimming squad first. Dancing would have to wait.

On Monday evenings I went with my brothers to the swimming squad training nights. It was sometimes tough – the other swimmers were older, taller, stronger, and therefore faster than me – but I was never last. I was never a failure on Monday night swimming, I was just the youngest. I was the smallest and therefore, by default, the weakest.

Monday evening always brought me relief. Monday evening, I was like a different person. I knew I was still me, but somehow other people saw a different me and I never stopped to ask why. I just looked forward to Monday night swimming club. They liked me – more to the point, they liked me for being me. They wanted to be in my company, or at least did not protest me being in theirs. They wanted me to be on their team. They wanted me, they included me, they told me I tried hard, they rewarded me for my efforts. They weren't disappointed that someone said they had to spend time with me. They weren't ashamed of me, or more accurately ashamed of themselves for having to spend time in my company.

No one at swimming club knew how stupid I was; they did not ask and did not care. What mattered on Monday nights was that I tried my hardest. I actually tried my hardest during school work too, but what made Monday nights different was that the trainer saw and acknowledged my efforts.

Training on Monday night was a mixed bag. We did medley relays, leg training, arm training, breathing exercises, sighting underwater, stroke counting, and tumble turn after tumble turn. It was hard work but I was equal to the others, even though most of them were older, taller, faster kids. I was Rhona

Macdonald, pretty quick for her age. My current times were compared to my previous times, not to times set by the older members of the group or the teacher's expectations or parental expectations. It was a fair contest, one not rigged by how the teacher felt. It was within my grasp to beat my previous time. It gave me a chance at success.

We finished every training with an all-ages race. Four people would be picked and they would take turns picking the rest. I was never last picked, even though I was the youngest. I held my breath, willing to hear my name, and when it came I swam across to my team with pride. The race changed each week: sometimes it would be each person had to do a fifty-metre freestyle, other times it was a fifty-metre medley and we had to sort out who was doing which stroke. Sometimes our team won, sometimes we didn't, but it was fun either way. We always cheered and laughed and held our breaths. We all won. I always went home exhausted and hungry and longing for the next Monday.

Yes, I would learn to walk again, then swim, then dance.

I hopped along holding on to whatever was handy: furniture, rails, and even walls. I resembled an old woman simply trying to get from here to there without falling, although I was going to improve and the old woman would likely get worse.

I did get better, although my leg was still weak.

I took a risk one night and enquired over dinner whether I was going to be allowed to continue into Primary Seven, and my parents confirmed that I was through. It did not matter what score I got in the end of year tests. They could not go back on their word – my whole family were my witnesses.

I actually looked forward to test week. It was a week of no homework and little class work. It was a week of silence, no teachers shouting and no kids giggling, no one sitting at clever

Chapter 21

or daft tables. Everyone sat by themselves, facing the same way with the same test paper in peace and quiet. Everyone was equal, at least until the papers were gathered and marked. The test papers were always multiple choice, so I could at least keep up.

The teacher's speech that preceded test week was unchanged from year to year. I never gave it much attention; it wasn't practical or even useful to me. "Take your time, read every word of every question, read all the answers before choosing your answer." I never understood their closing statement: "If you cheat, you're only cheating yourself."

The timing for turning pages was the first and most valuable of my tools, a technique I had perfected over the years. I turned the pages in time with everyone else. The clever kids always started the turn first, and while I knew not to turn the page with them it was a cue to get ready. Then there would be a rush of the average clever people turning their pages, and I would turn my page once the rush of that group was over but before the stragglers started their turning. I had to turn before the stragglers, not because I thought I was cleverer than them – I knew I wasn't – but because sometimes the clever turners would be ready to turn again before the stragglers had finished their turn, sort of like being lapped in a race. I had to pace myself to be just behind the middle group so that I wouldn't lead, which would clearly demonstrate I was cheating by not reading the questions, nor fall behind, demonstrating my stupidity. I could at least dream of being average and turn the page with the majority. Father always said there was safety in numbers.

In Primary Three, I enjoyed the tranquillity and rhythm of checking a box for each question: A, B, C, D, E, or F. Simple, easy, finished. The results would show the same as they always did: that I had not read a single question. I denied the accusation from the teacher, even though it was true. I knew my error – the results had not shown her that I'd not read a single question, her eyes had told her. She had watched me and caught on to what I was doing. I had to change my strategy.

I abandoned my timed turnings briefly and tried to read every question, but doing this meant that I never finished, never even came close. Reading every second question turned out to be too time-consuming and too easy for the marker to work out what I was doing. The best method, and one I stuck with for a few years, was to read random questions in the time between turns, sometimes a few in a row. This resulted in all questions getting answered, no traceable rhythm to reading or not reading, and of course a final mark that was expected by the teacher and myself, and which would secure me a seat at the daft table the following year.

When the test week for Primary Six ended I celebrated in knowing that I made it through to the final round, the final year of primary school, no matter what the scores were. I owed my broken leg a lot. I owed it my life, and my sanity; my survival was only due to this event. The next teacher could not be as bad, could she? Surely there was not worse.

22

On top of the Rory I used to visit next door, another Rory I visited during the school holidays was an almost-white golden retriever. Rory lived in a massive house with my uncle and auntie, one I used to explore when I was a lot younger. The house was never filled with children as I had once predicted. When everyone laughed at me and said something about my uncle, my mother's brother, and his wife, my auntie, being older than Mum, I didn't understand why. I had been their flower girl at their wedding, but I don't remember the event. That's another photo.

I loved my week with Rory in Cruden Bay; I know this because I don't recall those weeks in great detail. My brain never seemed to retain happy memories. My uncle was an oil man, his work based in the Aberdeen offices, while my auntie worked part time at the local Links golf club. When I got up in the morning there would be nobody in the house other than Rory, who would be sleeping in his room off the kitchen which he shared with the washing machine. The only noise would be the radio, which was always left on to keep him company. It was peaceful.

I would stay in the cosy kitchen and get some toast and

juice as noisily as I could. I wanted to wake Rory, but I knew I should never wake a dog in case they were in the middle of a bad dream. Rory was easy to wake, though, and he would come out of his room quickly. He liked toast, but he had a delicate stomach and I didn't want to make him ill so I never gave him much. His meals of chicken and rice were much better for him anyway.

Once he was awake, I would sit with Rory, patting him down his shoulder and telling him my troubles. He was a brilliant listener so long as you kept the pats coming. He often turned his head and squinted his eye as if to say, "Really, that happened? You should be a dog, sleeping all day in your own room with the radio going and chicken on its way." The hourly radio news would tell us that latest prisoner to escape from Scotland's gulag – Peterhead Prison, the prison of no hope – was still on the run. Rory never showed any worry about the situation, so neither did I. I recall Mum talking to my uncle and auntie about the criminal, and I presumed the criminal worried her. After all, if I did not go to school then she too would be a criminal and be taken away to Peterhead Prison.

Rory was too strong for me to walk by myself, but when my aunt came home we would walk him together, usually round by the ruined castle. Rory loved water and frequently ran away down the cliff for a quick swim, even if it was blowing a gale and my auntie was telling him not to.

My auntie would ask about school on these walks, but it was never the main topic of conversation. My uncle, on the other hand, had more questions. He never asked all the questions all at once, but they were fundamentally the same. School, teacher, friends, best and worst subjects. I always gave the correct answers as they led to fewer follow-up questions.

Some evenings we would play Scrabble, which was not my

Chapter 22

board game of choice, but because my uncle and aunt did not have children they did not have as a many board games as we did. My uncle and I would start. I never concentrated on placing words for the score, but instead on placing words that were hopefully spelt correctly. My auntie would come and join us after tidying up after dinner, and she would always place the letters on my little board into a word that I never saw. My uncle would sometimes say "Hey, no cheating," or "Don't gang up against me," so I would wait a few rounds then place the newly found word on the board. My uncle never caught us, or if he did he never felt the need to shame me and my auntie about cheating. Or rather, "working together," as I was ready to claim if the accusation was ever voiced.

I'm not sure if I ever won a game, even with my auntie's help, but for once I did not hate letters or words. Nonetheless, I was pleased when the nine o'clock chime came to signal it was time for me to go to bed. Off I'd go, full of another life, one that was not filled by school, and when I woke up it would be just Rory and me again.

23

Primary Seven started out much better than Primary Six. My teacher turned out to be the lady who had helped when I was stranded without my wooden supports. She had waited with me until I corrected their height. She even opened the door and protected me from the witch's outburst that I knew would have shown itself if I'd arrived alone. I liked her; she had been kind to me.

Could she be kind for a year? Would I be that lucky?

I *was* that lucky. Miss Primary Seven never shouted at me. In fact, she never really shouted at anyone. Her classroom was fairly quiet, so quiet I could sometimes hear my former teacher shouting at the new pupils under her guard. I froze every time until I reassured myself that I wasn't in her class any more. I had escaped her grasp.

I still attended the retard class; it was a calm place where I never got shouted at. It was almost safe. I say almost because the second I relaxed and believed myself to be safe, something would change. But as I don't recall any major incidents, or indeed recall much at all about my time in this special class, this room must have been safe.

This year, I was also finally able to prove to my classmates

Chapter 23

that I could dance. During our local Highland Games, I won Best Local Dancer and was presented with a cup. As usual, I wasn't allowed to take the cup to school to parade it around the other rooms to prove that I could dance. If I had been allowed, I would have announced during every class I visited that I had beaten the two younger show-off girls who used to parade their little trophies, that they wouldn't be around today because I'd beaten them. That I was first.

I wasn't allowed to take the trophy, but the local paper put photo of me and my cup on the front page – the cup looked as big as me. I took the paper in my bag, ready to produce it if anyone ever said I couldn't dance. I was armed. I was ready to defend myself. I could dance. In fact, I was the best local dancer, even though I only had a black and white photo to prove it. I never did have to show it to anyone, but I kept the paper with me as a secret weapon against those who may question me.

My teacher was nicer this year, but I still wasn't good at school. My Primary Seven teacher asked us once to draw a picture of a well-known saying that when taken at face value did not show what we as humans understood it to mean. She gave the example of "it's raining cats and dogs." We had to think of another saying and draw it.

I wondered if I had already done this task in Primary Four with my Goldilocks and the sodding three bears. I couldn't think of another saying that wasn't what it said. I wasn't very sure what she meant by well-known sayings, but I didn't want to ask since she had spent so much time explaining the task and everyone around me was already in action.

I think we were to come up with incorrect sayings that were understood to be something else, like raining cats and dogs. It was never going to rain cats and dogs, it was always just going to be heavy rain, but rain is not heavy so it's not really heavy rain either. Clothing is heavy once it is wet by rain, so it should be "it's heavy clothes weather," but that wasn't how the saying went.

I recognised I was going round in circles. Another incorrect saying. I was sitting perfectly still, I was not going round in circles. My brain was not even going round in circles. So, the saying going round in circles meant I don't understand, I'm stuck. I couldn't draw circles though, and what if we had to stand up and explain our pictures? I'd get tongue-tied. There, another incorrect saying, and another I would not be drawing.

"Good morning" was a well-known saying that taken on face value was incorrect; mornings were never good. "Face value" was un-drawable so had to be discarded. "Sleep tight, don't let the bed bugs bite" wasn't true in our house as we didn't have bed bugs, but it was possible that other houses did. I believed the kids in Africa were starving but doubted they'd eat cold, lumpy custard either, so I could not use that. I thought of "too cold to snow" but had no idea how to draw it. Weather was hard to draw. Rain is just rain; whether it's heavy or a drizzle, it just looks like rain, and frost looks the same as snow. You can't even see ice or damp, so how could you draw them?

My mother used to always say "it will end in tears" a lot, or if she was cross with us she would say "I'll get the stick," but I didn't know if these were just sayings in our home or if everyone's mothers said them. Besides, they were true a lot of the time, especially the latter one.

One of Evan's teachers had told him that he'd have to pull up his socks, which Evan duly did. Everyone had laughed, even Mum when he recited the story later to ask what he had done wrong. Seemingly, the teacher had meant that he would have to try harder – why not just say that? They said that to me all the time.

Chapter 23

The more I thought about these sayings, the more I did not like them. They seemed like they were out to get you, to make you look silly. I recall that I had done something correct – when told I had an Uncle Bob, I corrected that person and informed them I did not have an Uncle Bob, I had an Uncle Donald and Uncle Sandy and an uncle through marriage named David. They all laughed and the thing I had done correctly was immediately lost in my stupidity of not acknowledging my not-Uncle Bob.

These sayings were lies. It would be so much easier if people just said what they meant, but people don't, so I would have to learn and be ready for these not-funny lies.

All my teachers said they were trying to help me, and that was another incorrect saying. The witch from the year before should have said on day one, "I don't like you, Rhona. I'm going to pick on you every opportunity I get. I will humiliate you every day. You will fear me even when you are not in my class." Instead, she said she would do everything she could to help me learn.

Repeating Primary Three will boost my confidence – lie. Sucking lead pencils will kill you – lie. They only do it because they care – lie. You don't need to go to the toilet – lie. What doesn't break you makes you stronger – lie. The teacher told us time was half way – possible fact. I'd not even started.

I really liked dogs and I knew I could draw them. I even knew the saying meant it was raining really heavily so I would be able to explain it, if that turned out to be the trick to this task. She had already written it on the board, so I knew I could spell it. I started drawing mostly dogs with a few badly-drawn cats.

We had to put our pictures on the wall, just like the nursery rhyme, and then we discussed what the saying meant. I was safe – my cats weren't drawn well, but the dogs would make up for it. I rehearsed what I'd say, explaining that I did not have a cat so could not really draw them, but then remembered I did not have a dog either so that justification was not valid. Maybe I'd just not mention the badly-drawn cats, which now actually just looked like small dogs. I had a picture of dogs of different sizes falling from the fake sky, landing unharmed on a grey payment. If dogs had really fallen from the sky, they would have been hurt on impact. My drawing was wrong. I'd used the example the teacher had given us and drawn magical dogs of different sizes flying around a blue and grey background.

Then it was my turn.

I stood up with my picture (true).

I explained that I'd drawn "it's raining cat and dogs" (lie).

The teacher said the class were to guess what the drawing was of, from what I'd drawn. I must not have heard her say that earlier (true, I had been rehearsing what I was going to say, I never heard anything of the ten or so people that went before me).

Some smelly kid shouted out "It's raining cats and dogs" (lie, and I'd just said that. Maybe he wasn't listening and thought himself really smart).

She asked why I chose that saying.

I said because my parents say it all the time when it's raining really hard (lie, they didn't say that).

She asked what it meant.

I explained that it meant that it was raining really heavily, again.

There was a pause, a long pause.

She wanted more, not necessarily from me, I remained standing, silent, lost in thought.

Then she said thank you and I sat down, and the next person

Chapter 23

stood up beside a horrifying picture. There was a mixing bowl with some hands skinning eyes, and there was blood everywhere. Her picture meant to pay close attention. I could not understand why "keep your eyes peeled" would make you see better. So that was a good lie.

Another horror picture was someone eating – or, after discussion which I took no part in, biting – a bullet; that one was to make a confession. Bite the bullet – lie. I did not like these lies. It was like everyone knew all these were lies apart from me, and maybe my brother.

Someone drew a washing basket on a case; this turned out to be a stupid person, but just like we can't say "nigger" any longer, we have to call stupid people "mentally ill." No one needed me in these discussions about deception and lies, so my mind drifted off to happier things. One more year. Soon, this might be over. Or so I thought.

This final year contained a lot of talking. We had a discussion following most class tasks about moving from being the seniors in primary school to the juniors of secondary school, about potential bullying and what to do. How was I only hearing about this now? This should have been explained on day one of primary. I have already lived the life my Primary Seven teacher was explaining. How bad was secondary going to be?

There was talk about the different patterns of subjects. In secondary school I would have several teachers throughout the year, even several throughout any day. This was great news. The teacher's pets would have to work extra hard to be all the teachers' pets. When one teacher picked on me, I would not have to wait a year for another chance; I would only have to wait an hour or so.

There was also lots of talking after the sex education videos. These videos reported that if someone was "bulling you," which was calling you names and making fun of you, making you feel bad, then they were actually attracted to you. Another helpful member of the class pointed this out to the policeman's son, and after that I was never chased home or called poison again. I wish we could have had sex education a few years before.

On a farm and raspberry jam visit a few years ago, I had been outside and saw two hens fighting. I had gone rushing into the farmhouse and reported that one hen was on top of another and that the one on the bottom was in pain and needed help. My grandma, uncle, mother, and father all laughed at me and told me they were playing, but I was not quietened. I repeated that the bottom hen was not enjoying the game and that it needed help. My father got up and we went looking for the playing/fighting hens, but we never found them. I was sure the bottom hen was hiding. Father assured me it would be okay, that what doesn't kill you makes you stronger, and we went back inside for more pancakes and raspberry jam while I worried that the bottom hen had been killed rather than becoming stronger. Now I realise they were having sex, and the adults' laughs were at me and my lack of understanding, and they filled me with lies instead of telling me they were making a baby. Whether their lies were correctly placed, I do not know. Their laughter was not.

I used to talk a lot, and I mean a lot, most of which was nonsense. My life was boring, so I'd take something that actually happened and change it a little or a lot to make that event sound more interesting to my audience. Silence was not my friend; silence led to my mind overworking, overturning the facts of my miserable life. Silence ended in a downward spiral of the shit events of my life, both the ones in past and the ones I envisaged in the future. I thought it better to add a little spice to life and chat to whoever would listen.

Chapter 23

I didn't talk much in class, although many of my teachers would likely disagree with that statement. Experience taught me that talking in school got me into trouble, either for talking in class or talking a different language than I was writing. When it was quiet in class, my mind freestyled into its downwards spiral.

I listened to everyone talk about secondary school, and I wondered what my life would be like next year. I held on to the small glimmer of hope that secondary school couldn't possibly be as bad as primary school. I did my best to keep my mind out of that downward spiral.

24

As 1988 came to a close, I realized that this year had turned out to be a not-so-bad year for me. I wasn't held back in Primary Six, I was no longer called poison, it was now accepted that I could dance, the teacher did not shout constantly, and there was the hope of secondary school to look forward to.

However, 1988 was a not-so-good year for Scotland.

That summer, an event occurred that changed Scotland Rigging forever. I remember wandering through the quiet house that night, unable to sleep. My parents were sat in the living room. I sat by my father and he let me sip his whisky – it never tasted better like he said it would, it always burnt my throat. He was watching the ten o'clock news, just as he had watched the nine o'clock news and the six o'clock news, as if anything would change substantially within those three hours. On that night, though, he got lucky. The ten o'clock news was interrupted, by news. A North Sea rig had exploded. My uncle never actually worked on the North Sea rigs thankfully, he was a suited man in an office. There were a few men in our town who worked the fortnight-on, fortnight-off routine. Father had seen our next-door neighbour, Mr Bilbo, in the afternoon, so he was on a fortnight off.

Chapter 24

I watched the news with my parents. Evan had come from his room into the living room, and even Mother was paying attention now. The rig was on fire, a huge red and orange blaze against the pitch-black night. The footage was taken from a helicopter, with radio chatter in the background. Reports came that the rescue boats and helicopter couldn't get close. The gas lines ruptured, causing more fireballs and more destruction. The rig was to be lost to the North Sea. It wasn't really going to be lost – the rig would be at the bottom of the North Sea. Just another silly lie.

I wanted to see the sea engulf the rig, but I woke up in the morning in my own bed. The rig was still burning, with an unknown number of lives lost; again, not lost. They didn't want to say dead, although that was the truth. North Sea rigging would never be the same again.

By the end of the Thursday, the death toll was 164 lives. Those who survived did so because they jumped from the rig's helicopter pad into the North Sea – jumping seemed to offer a better chance of living than staying on the rig, and they wanted to stay alive. By the end of the week, burn specialists were flying into Aberdeen to treat the severe burns on the lucky survivors of the biggest oil field disaster in history.

This explosion wasn't the only disaster that year. Just before Christmas, the world became aware of a town not much bigger than Grantown for a very unfortunate reason. Pan Am flight 103, on the London to New York leg of its journey, fell out of the sky from 31,000 feet and made a crater within the town of Lockerbie.

Before Christmas arrived, it became clear that the flight had been bombed. There were several different groups claiming the work. Everyone felt sorry for the victims, both the passengers on the flight and the residents of Lockerbie, and the time of year seemed to make it worse. I wondered if our town lay 31,000 feet under a flight path. Might there be a chance that this could happen to me? I knew better than to ask.

Everyone was pleased that 1988 was over; everyone apart from me. This year had turned out okay, but I didn't know what the next year would be like. I wanted to stay in this moment forever, this moment where I could say my teacher was okay, that my year was okay. I didn't know if I'd ever be able to say this again.

25

With the new year came new excitement. We went to the secondary school for a day visit, which confirmed everything my Primary Seven teacher and brother had said. The clever kids in the class were not as pleased with the upcoming changes as I was, and some said they feared being bullied. I knew what they really feared was the lack of power and control, which is very different from the fear of being bullied. I told myself that nothing could be as bad as the last few years, and I only had to do a few more before I could legally run off without Mother being taken away.

Evan would be in Secondary Five when I would join Secondary One. Evan liked secondary school, or at least he never said he didn't like it. The older children were usually the bullies, or so we were told by the real bullies: the teachers. I did not fear being bullied. There was no segregation of males and females, so I could seek out Evan or his friends if needed. I would potentially have several bullies to deal with in any given day, but I would not have to cope with one bully all day every day for a year. I did not fear secondary school.

The new year also brought a very unexpected surprise. When I arrived home after school one day, Mother told me not to get excited, so I instantly got excited. She explained that she had been reading the Press and Journey Paper and there was a listing for Old English Sheepdog puppies for sale. I stood frozen on the spot – did this mean she and Dad had changed their minds? Was I going to get my longed-for puppy? I was frightened to ask, and she was still talking anyway. She had already called the number that was listed in the paper and spoken with the breeder. There were three girls available; there were also two boys, but they had already been sold. I was still too frightened/excited as to what might be said next to ask anything – it felt like I'd been holding my breath since I got home. The breeder and therefore the puppies were in Aberdeen-Shire, which was a two-hours' drive from our home in Grantown. She had spoken to Dad, and he was finishing work and coming home early so we could go.

The weather forecast had predicted a winter storm and the skies were already darkening, indicating the forecaster would be correct in his prediction. Dad would decide if we were going to see the puppies once he got home, but I got everything ready in case he said yes. I found a box in the garage that the puppy could sit in and Mum found some old bedding I could use.

Evan was next home from school and Mum went through the story again. She said that Calum would not be coming home, he did not live with us anymore. He was grown up and moved out, and somehow this meant that we could now have a dog. Now Evan and I were both ready and waiting for Father to arrive home and declare if we were going to look at the puppies.

He duly arrived, saw my box, and announced that we better get going. He told us to get ready, that we needed to get as many miles done as possible before the storm hit. Mum, Evan and I were ready; it was only Dad that had to change out of his

Chapter 25

work clothes. Evan and I had our box and bedding in the car before Dad was changed. We set off in near darkness at 4:00 p.m., and Evan and I spent the drive explaining the benefits of having a dog. We did not have enough justification to fill the time, so I repeated the few facts we had. I volunteered my responsibilities of dog ownership, the training, the walking, the feeding, the visits to the vet, and the grooming – which with an Old English Sheepdog would be huge. The dog would be my best friend, my only friend. I would even practice reading aloud to my dog.

Two hours later, we were in Aberdeen-Shire. It was pitch black and steadily raining, without a star or a moon to light the sky. As per the instructions that Mum had received from the breeder, we turned off the road by the big oak tree, went one and a half miles up the drive, and arrived at the farm.

There were indeed three girls: a big one, a medium one, and small one. We went out with the breeder and spent time with all of them, and they were all adorable. The big one was busy running between the cattle's legs while the little one seemed quite timid and shied away from everyone. The medium one bounced between her sisters and us, looking for all the attention that was on offer. Mum and Dad were finished talking to the breeder and announced that the choice was mine. This would be my dog. I would be responsible for its wellbeing, so I was responsible for picking which pup I wanted to take home. I chose the middle one, steering clear of the possible runt of the litter and the boisterous big one.

After money was exchanged for the pedigree papers and my pup, we commenced the return journey home. The rain was thick now, with wipers going double time. The little puppy spent a maximum of two minutes in the box; the rest of the time, Evan and I shared her. She was sick and spent a penny or two on us, but we didn't care. She was coming home with us.

Once we got home, the little pup investigated her new house. It was now really late and we were all tired. The pup got locked in the kitchen overnight, and I went to sleep listening to her yelp and cry.

The next day was Saturday, which meant we could spend the day with our new pup. She had shredded her paper and spent many pennies in her prison of the kitchen, but she was full of kisses and fun once we released her into the garden. Mr Bilbo came to congratulate me and see the new pup, and he deemed her to have big paws.

Evan and Mum went to Inverness to get some food bowls and a bed for the pup while I stayed at home and commenced my dog ownership responsibilities. Dada had gone to work to finished up stuff he had not been able to do the day before. I took my pup into the garden very five minutes, waited until she spent a penny, and took her back in. Then I took her out every ten minutes, waited until she relieved herself, and took her back in. By the end of the day she knew that she was to wee outside, and all accidents that occurred happened when she was locked in the kitchen overnight.

I had never been good at naming animals. Evan had suggested Thumper for my silver fox black boxing rabbit, and he now suggested Kerry for the pup. So, she was named Kerry.

Kerry turned out to be the best dog ever, although not too smart. I walked her every day after school without fail. Evan walked her most evenings, and Mum kept her company during the day while we were at school. Kerry always gave me a huge welcome when I got home and then we'd set out for our walk, rain or shine or anything in between. I groomed her most days and fed her the required amount of meals as she grew. I took her for her regular visits to the vet and kept her vaccinations up to

Chapter 25

date, and Kerry never complained. When Evan and I watched TV, she would fall asleep and we'd giggle at her hiccups as she slept.

She was always upset at being locked in the kitchen overnight and would spend hours crying before settling down to sleep. Then, one night Mum needed something that was in the dining room, which could only be entered through the kitchen. Kerry was still crying at being locked in so Mum did not think it would make thing worse to go in and get what she needed. She opened the door and Kerry shot out and up into my bedroom, where she curled into a tight ball on her bed. Mum noticed Kerry has already soiled the paper in the kitchen, so Kerry was granted a trial overnight stay in my room. If she soiled the bed, she would have to go back into the kitchen until she could hold her bladder overnight. Kerry would never spend another night crying herself to sleep in the kitchen.

Ever since the winter's night I chose her from between the cattle feet, she was my best friend – my only friend. I never asked my parents why they had changed their minds, and the answer did not matter. I finally had my long-awaited, long-dreamed-of dog, and I was happy.

26

I only had a few months left of primary school. Evan had long since survived primary school; he also had not found this time to be "the best years of his life." He had his own battles in trying to understand what the teachers wanted from him, but he conformed and complied just enough to ensure he never spent any time in the special classroom. There was no chatter that he would benefit from being held back.

In fact, there was never much chatter from Evan in general. When he was in Primary Five – I was in Primary One at the time – his teacher realized Evan was deaf, which came as quite a shock to our parents. I just thought what my parents had thought: that he was simply stubborn. This diagnosis made sense to me though. He never had the strawberry medicine because he did not hear our parents explaining how it would cure his lurgy. He saw us all having some and must have thought it was an optional item, like a sweet jar where you take one and pass it on. On our caravanning journeys, he never moved from the middle seat when the time came because he never heard or understood the rule that we all move every thirty minutes. He did not understand why we were moving and got tired, so he simply decided to sit still. He never heard Calum and I

Chapter 26

quarrelling that we both now wanted to sit in the middle. It made perfect sense Evan was deaf. Evan's world was quiet and peaceful; he wasn't hearing the demands and threats made by everyone around him.

But how had nobody noticed that he was deaf in his first nine years of life? None of his previous teachers noticed anything other than a quiet boy who kept to himself, but his Primary Five teacher noticed he never answered her questions or carried out her instructions. He never turned his head to see who was receiving the most recent verbal correction, and he never even flinched when the verbal correction was directed at him. He could talk, although he frequently chose not to.

Evan didn't seem deaf to me – he answered my questions, although he did also ignore some of my questions. He didn't chat away like I did, he only spoke when he needed to. His primary school teachers were no better than mine, but teachers are always correct. And so, eight weeks later Evan went with our parents to see the specialist for confirmation and to find out what the next steps were, for him and for us as a family. I did not get to go, likely in case I told a doctor a truth that was not meant to be told. I had to go to school instead.

The specialist did not confirm Evan's deaf diagnosis. He did, however, confirm that Evan's hearing was one hundred percent perfect. Evan could hear everything and everyone, including his Primary Five teacher. Evan simply chose not to hear her; he chose not to react. He went back to school, back to ignoring her, back to not doing whatever class work he chose, back to letting her shout and scream and not even flinching. Nothing changed, but Evan's hearing was tickety-boo; it was perfect. He had created a quiet, safe world for himself, and he spent countless hours in it. I wanted in, or I wanted my own version.

His Primary Six teacher had also been concerned, but not

about his hearing – although his hearing capabilities were revisited many times as an explanation to Evan's apparent peaceful living. Instead, Evan's Primary Six teacher was concerned about Evan's inability to do basic mathematics. She spent many a break time explaining and re-explaining math problems to Evan. He sat with her and watched her do and redo the problems, but when faced with more math problems in actual class, he would put down his pencil and fail to solve any of them. This then led to him missing more play time to watch her solve these math problems again, and again, and again. He failed maths term, after term, after term.

He went on to secondary school where he liked the physics teacher, and where he liked physics. In Primary Six he was unable to complete basic math, but in secondary school he was top in both his math and physics classes. There was now discussion about how clever he was, how the maths teachers in the secondary school could not teach him anything more. It turns out that he never did his primary school maths because it bored him; he felt it was a better use of his time to hide himself away in his quiet, safe world.

I dearly hoped for a similar fate – to one day discover that I was in truth so clever at something that the basics just hadn't been worth my time. I began to dream of it between dreaming that death would seek me out faster.

The rest of Primary Seven was uneventful, and soon enough it was over. I had survived primary school, and after the summer holidays I would be in Secondary One. I only had to make it through a few more years of "the best years of my life," and then I would be free.

Part Two
The Bridge

27

Scotland, 1989

After five months in secondary school, I knew my way around without the map my brother had helped me draw after my first day. The school, which was called Grantown Grammar, had swelled in numbers as all the pupils of the outlying village primary schools were now bussed in to continue their education. There were three hundred pupils across the six years, and the classes had a similar number of pupils to any of my previous primary classes – about thirty in each. I liked how not everyone in every class knew that I was the class idiot in primary. I was not deranged to the unfamiliar classmates, at least not yet. I knew it would become apparent soon enough that I was the class idiot, but for the first wee while I could act normal.

I liked the rhythm of the grammar school. We changed class every forty or sixty minutes, and we had several teachers on any given day. There was no time for the primary school teacher's pet to be all the teachers' pets in all the classes, a notion which was confirmed when Mum said she had met a parent of one of the former pets and reported that he did not like Grammar School. He did not like the constant change, but I did. There

Chapter 27

was structure, with a set pattern to the classes. I knew how long I would be doing a given task or subject – it was dictated by the school bell ringing, not the teacher's state of mind. I had subjects that I did not like and teachers that I did not trust, but I could tick my survival off by forty or sixty minute slots. This was far more achievable than the never-ending years of primary.

The bell rang, indicating the change of classes, and I moved from geography to English. I did not dislike either subject, and both teachers seemed to have a stable temperament. As I found my seat, I noticed there were two bits of paper face-down on everyone's tables. This was unusual; I wondered what was going to unfold.

Miss English announced that today's lesson was a mock test, and my day went pear-shaped in a heartbeat. My stomach plummeted into my bowels, which instantly started churning. My hands were clammy as I started to silently panic. I wasn't ready for a test. She hadn't said there was to be test at the end of last class, I would have remembered. How had I not remembered? I was going to have to escape to the bathroom.

Miss English started to explain how the test would go. I tried to pay attention as there were often hints in verbal explanations that I never saw in written explanations. On one piece of paper there were a list of questions, and on the other was a passage that held the answers to the questions. It was really hot; I pushed up my sleeves. I felt nauseous. Was I going to be sick?

She instructed us to turn the papers over. I was taking deep breaths now, wiping my hands on my skirt, deciding if I was going to be sick or needed to go to the bathroom. *This is a bloody shamble*, I thought. I'd only been at this school for thirty seconds – I had years to endure yet.

She started talking again, and I realized she was reading the passage. I looked at the paper in front of me and confirmed she was indeed reading the words, and she was on the second line. I looked up at her and she was staring right at me. Staring right through me, probably knowing that I'd not been keeping up for the first two lines. I looked back down and followed the words as she continued to read clearly, evenly-paced, naturally, her breathing steady, her voice calm, emphasising some of the words. It was like a beautiful song. Not even in my wildest dreams did I envisage myself ever being able to read like that. I followed along, permitting my eyes a fraction of an extra second on words she presented with extra tone – my mind knew these were maybe the keys words, and that these words were worth remembering. When she had finished the passage, she read out the questions. I followed those words as well.

When there was nothing left for her to read, she asked us to re-read the passage on our own and then answer the questions. We had until the end of class to complete the task.

The passage was all too fresh in my mind to confuse my head by trying to re-read it. She had read it perfectly – I knew what it said. My re-reading it would not add anything positive to my understanding. So, I moved straight to the questions and began writing answers, breaking my own set rule. I was first to start writing, completely and utterly out of timing with my classmates who I was usually so careful to keep pace with in order to avoid being highlighted as different. As I answered the questions, I looked back at the passage to locate certain words. Several were the recently emphasized words, so my eyes knew exactly where to find them.

I wasn't the first finished, but I did answer all the questions before the bell went. Then we all got up and headed to our next class.

Although I did not have my usual preparation time, we

Chapter 27

would get our results at the next English lesson so I did have ample time for my post-test self-prosecution. I had learned that if I thought something was easy then I had done it wrong, as I had surely misunderstood the task. If I thought it was hard, I'd failed as usual. And if I thought it was really difficult, I could start preparing for being at the bottom of the class again. This time would be no different, and I only had two days to wait to be proven correct once more. The Chinese Whispers would start, and then everything would be horrible again.

Two days later we were back in English. Miss English stood by the blackboard and wrote spots for first, second, and third place along the side – thankfully, she was not inclined to write up second to last and last, so I would be saved from mortification on this occasion.

The usual name was written as first place: the boy who disrupted all my classes, the one who answered back to every teacher. The boy who constantly interrupted and never listened to instructions. He who never did his homework. The boy who got his name written up by first place in math, English, history, and geography. The boy I hated. The boy I wanted to be. The boy who was living proof that God could not possibly exist and there was likely no afterlife – that this is it, this is your life, and that your school years are the best years of your life. Life is so unfair. What is the point of life? What is the point of even trying to compete? I had lost before I even began.

Miss English wrote my name on the board beside second place.

Time stopped. I sat gobsmacked, unable to move, unable to breathe, unable to think. Everyone was looking at me, everyone wondering the same: "How?" Someone had the answer, and it gained strength as it rippled through the class. I had cheated. But how was that possible? The boy who was first was sat on the other side of the room from me.

Miss English demanded silence, said, "Very well done, Rhona," and moved on to writing up the third-place-getter, who also thankfully sat too far away to have enabled my copying.

Miss English moved on with the lesson, an overview of the questions and correct answers, but I was still confused as to how this second place could have happened.

I must have cheated. It's true, I cheated with such regularity sometimes that my eyes would be straining to read others' work to the left or right or even upside down. My eyes cheated before my brain knew they were. But how had I cheated on this occasion?

Miss English must have made an error in her marking, or was this her little joke? Was this how secondary school teachers highlighted the daft ones, by building them up to knock them down? That could be really, really bad for me. That was a rollercoaster I did not want to be strapped into.

I was scaring myself now. What if all the rules I had learned in primary were now null and void? What if there was a whole new set to learn? I knew I wasn't listening, my mind was running out of control. If she asked me anything now, my reply would be silence. I put on my best calm "I don't care" face. Usually it was the "I don't care, you won't make me cry" face, but the same face worked for concealing excitement. My name remained on the blackboard beside second place all class. I checked it a thousand times.

The bell went, class was finished. We filed out. My name remained by second place, her error uncorrected, her punchline undelivered. I let the glory of second warm me and settle in my stomach while ensuring my "I don't care" face remained unchanged. While second place was usually a mark of failure in my household, it was a massive leap from my usual second-last

Chapter 27

placement. And, as an extra prize, my eyes had apparently developed a new way of long-distance cheating and kept it a secret from my brain.

I shared my second-place glow with Mother when I got home, but she already knew. In fact, my father was also home, changing out of his work clothes into what my mother called "presentable clothes," which she had of course taken out of the cupboard in preparation as if to say "you will change into these." The punchline was delivered by my parents: Miss English had been in contact, and my parents were off to an emergency meeting at the school. I tried to reassure them that I had not cheated (it was impossible, they sat too far away!) but off they went.

I curled up safe in bed. I convinced myself that I was confident I had not cheated, and that my eyes had not betrayed my ethic. Okay, I'd not entirely followed the instructions on the test day, but that wasn't cheating. I fell asleep, my mind's eye revealing a blackboard. Second place: Rhona.

28

When my parents returned, Mum woke me with the verdict. Miss English did not think I had cheated. She thought I was mad, or at least possibly suffering from a brain disorder called dyslexia. I'd never heard of this mental disorder, and I doubted my parents had either. I wasn't overly pleased, though my mother said it was a good thing – people could help me. She told me, "Don't worry, don't be scared, there's nothing to be afraid of," before leaving me still scared and now alone with my fear.

I was tired, cream-crackered tired. I didn't get up out of bed. I never had tea. I had to go and see Miss English tomorrow.

I didn't like the idea of a mental disorder, brain disorder, dyslexia. So what if people could help me? They wouldn't. I didn't want to live in Craig Dunain, the area's purpose-built lunatic asylum. I didn't want to be drugged. I didn't want to be fed liquidised food through a straw. Now I was mad as well as dim. Why me? Had I been so bad in a previous life? I laid in my bed and cried.

Mum came to see me in my bedroom, but I couldn't explain my woes. I knew she would likely promise that she would not send me away to Craig Dunain, but would that be the truth?

Chapter 28

There was no point in asking the question if I couldn't trust her answer.

My mother told me that one day when I was a baby, she was breastfeeding me when someone came to the front door and Father let them in. In her rush to move rooms so the visitor would not see her naked breast, she misjudged a doorway and hit my head, hard. I screamed a short, sharp, deep scream and then went back to suckling. She said she was frightened she had caused my brain injury.

I said nothing; there was nothing to say. I was now not only stupid, but also had a possible mental disorder and a brain injury. She stayed with me until I fell asleep. I so wanted her to leave me so I could eat my Do Not Eat canister.

The next morning the walk to school was long – no farther than any other day, but it took me ages. I didn't want to go, but I put one foot in front of the other towards my fate.

I went to see Miss English. She told me that having dyslexia meant I had a different way of learning than the other children. That being dyslexic did not mean I was less clever than anyone else, it just meant I learned differently. Dyslexic people often had above-average intelligence, she told me, they were just not very good at some tasks like reading and spelling. Sometimes they mixed up left and right; sometimes they forgot what time it was or where they should be.

She told me the physicist Albert Einstein was dyslexic, and he had won a Nobel prize. The Scot, Alexander Graham Bell, inventor of the telephone, had been dyslexic. Actors Harrison Ford, Anthony Hopkins, and Tom Cruise were dyslexic. The Beatles songwriter John Lennon was dyslexic. Winston Churchill and John F. Kennedy were dyslexic. Famous writers Ernest Hemingway, F. Scott Fitzgerald, and William Butler Yeats all had dyslexia. Dyslexic people included surgeons, pioneers, explorers, comedians, artists, musicians. They were judges and lawyers – they were even astronauts.

But they were all males. How could I have a male disease?

She said Miss Math was dyslexic. Hmm, a teacher – that seemed a little less exciting than the men she had listed.

She offered Agatha Christie. She then explained that Agatha Christie had written novels, poems, and plays. She had written *Murder on the Orient Express*. That the *Guinness Book of World Records* lists Christie as the best-selling novelist of all time. That information was lodged.

She continued. Dyslexic people often understood more of what was spoken than what they read. Their handwriting was often not very neat, partly due to them trying to conceal their lack of confidence in their spelling. Their verbal vocabulary was far more extensive than their written vocabulary. Their listening vocabulary was greater still. They did not like reading aloud and tended to only read a word at a time with no fluency or emphasis, often ignoring punctuation.

I protested that I did not want to be mental. Everyone would tease me. No one in my family had ever been mental, it didn't run rampant in the family like cancer and heart disease did. Being mental would mean I would have to go and live in Craig Dunain, and, and, and, and, and… My mind had taken over once again.

Miss English's voice broke through my panic. She confirmed dyslexia was a mental health problem, but assured me it was not dementia. I would not be fed liquidised food through a straw when it got worse. My dyslexia would not, in fact, get worse, though it would not get better either. There was no cure.

Had I asked out loud about Craig Dunain? She gave no answer. Was that positive or negative?

I asked if I had had it in primary school. She said if I had

Chapter 28

dyslexia now, I would have had it in primary school too. I explained that all my teachers thought I was stupid. She disagreed and said that not all of my primary teachers thought so, but by default this confirmed that some did.

She said she thought I was very clever. That I had developed ways to help myself, and that I had a brilliant memory. She said she watched me during the recent test, and I never re-read the passage. I provided the answers from my memory while everyone else had to read and re-read the words.

She was the only teacher that ever said I was clever – she was well outnumbered by all the others. She must be wrong. She *was* wrong.

She spoke again. She'd been watching me since I arrived in her class. When we were reading aloud as a class she saw me trying to read a few lines ahead, trying to prepare for when I would be asked to read. She saw the fear creep across my body and saw me trying to suppress it. She saw me looking and focusing, heard me stumbling across the pronunciation of each word before moving to the next – each word spoken with no relation to the words beside it.

She said she thought I sat quietly not because I didn't have the answer in my head, but because I was frightened to say it in case I was wrong. She watched me copy from the blackboard, never looking directly at my paper but focusing on the words I was writing down and somehow still keeping those words in a straight line. She saw me copying from my neighbours, never moving my head away from its angle directed at my own paper, maintaining focus on one point as my eyes strained deeply to the right. She heard my stammer and overuse of "um" as I was buying myself time while my brain searched for my next spoken word.

She had talked to some of my other teachers. I always found

French and German hard because I couldn't hear the sounds of the parts of words. I couldn't hear them in English either. It wasn't that I hadn't learned them, my brain just couldn't hear them. I was trying to learn these languages by word association with English. Everyone tries to learn a foreign language this way to begin with, but then they give in to the sounds, at which point I had no option. My brain found sounding out words hard or impossible, a bit like how my brain didn't hear rhymes. The words had no connection for me.

If a teacher got angry with any other student in the class, I felt as if their anger and frustration were directed at me. I would freeze and remain frozen, unable to move or talk, unable to continue with whatever task was underway, as if willing myself to be somewhere, anywhere else. This paralysis was seen as drifting off, as not paying attention, which could actually draw attention to me and even redirect the teacher's anger.

So, she had spoken to Mr French and Miss German and Mr Biology. I wondered how many other teachers she had spoken to. Did they all know I might be mad?

Apparently, another teacher had noticed that I found it difficult to concentrate in a noisy classroom. If the class was split into groups doing different tasks, I could not even start my task if the other groups in the classroom were being loud. Background noise disrupted my thoughts and it took me a long time to get back to where I was before the disruption, which made me slow at my work.

With her diagnosis, I was numb. I felt exposed, my well-practiced survival methods uncovered and identified, aside from my little Do Not Eat canister. I was silent. I fought back tears.

Miss English said my teachers could change their teaching methods to help me learn, like reading a passage rather than

Chapter 28

making me read it myself, not asking me to read aloud, and not putting me on the spot. She said that if we could prevent the fear creeping in and hijacking my brain then I could absorb more, learn more, and that would lead me to become more confident.

She said she could help me. She said it didn't always have to be so hard for me. I so wanted to believe her that I let myself believe her. I agreed to the testing before I started crying. I was not sure if I wanted a positive or a negative answer, as both presented a minefield of problems that would later need to be navigated.

I made her promise not to tell anyone; I didn't want my class to know if I was mental.

Was it better to be simply stupid, or was it better to be stupid because you had a mental illness, a disease you couldn't spell? Did it really matter why you were stupid when the end result was the same? Was I just passing the blame on to dyslexia, my new and not-yet-understood friend? Was this part of myself I could simply un-invite into my life?

Could there be a cure for dyslexia? Medicine made breakthroughs all the time, so maybe if I was dyslexic it could be cured and then I might not have to be stupid. Or was that just stupid, to think I could be anything other than what I am?

29

The official testing day arrived.

There were two men in the testing room, a room that was hidden away beside the school's library. One man sat at a table and gestured me to sit beside him. The other man was sat in the corner behind me, where I couldn't see him from my seat. The one beside me said that the other chap was keeping an eye on him, but I knew he would be actually keeping an eye on me. I instantly mis-trusted this man; he had already lied.

He asked if I knew what a psychiatrist was and I said they were doctors who help people who didn't know how to help themselves, which he accepted as correct. Really, I knew that they were the doctors who locked up mental people into Craig Dunain. I would need to be on guard, as I was in real danger. I regretted agreeing to this testing.

Part of the testing was easy, stuff I'd done many times before. Hearing and seeing tests, as well as reading numbers that were hidden within a page full of little different-coloured circles. The psychiatrist had a huge stack of paper. He asked me to say whatever came into my head when I saw the picture on the paper, and then started turning the pages. I didn't always say the *very* first thing – instead, I said the first thing that would

Chapter 29

be acceptable, the first non-crazy thought that came into my head.

Next were words, single words in different text sizes, different fonts, and different text colours. I had to read them aloud. Then there were sentences and paragraphs.

The man would read something, then I had to read it back to him. He said a sentence and asked me to remember it. He asked me to read a sentence to him and then asked me to explain it. I repeated it, or at least repeated what I could remember of it.

He asked me to count the syllables in various words. I had never really understood this concept of syllables and as a result was never good at it. I'd always gone with what the majority had said in class, but here there was no class to ride with. So, I guessed. I knew that two and three were the most common. He started turning the stack of paper again. I looked at the length and guessed. We only did about five or six of the words. Maybe he moved onto the next thing as I'd got them all correct. I knew that was very unlikely, but there was no time to dwell on it – he was setting up the next task and asking me questions.

I had to read another sentence to him. He asked me to explain what the sentence was describing. I didn't know, but one of the words was "red" so I said it describes the colour red. I wondered whether I had done this test already, if maybe I was meant to repeat the sentence. But there was no time to think, he was moving quickly. I had to stay alert or he might recommend they lock me up.

"Which is your left hand?" he asked. I thought about it and held out my left hand. He asked me to say what went through my mind before I held out my hand. He was asking me what my trick was, to explain how I cheated.

I paused. He said he was here to help, that I was safe.

I knew I was in danger, but I was also trapped. Should I stand up and walk out, like I had not done in Primary One when I needed the toilet?

I couldn't stand up. I was beaten, again. I explained that I write with my right hand (I write with my write hand or I right with my right hand or I right with my write hand; English is funny if you forget the rules), so my other hand must be my left. I held out my imaginary pen in my right hand.

He asked me to say the alphabet starting anywhere other than A. I started at M. I had always wanted to start at O but got M and N the wrong way round, so I made my second alphabet start at M. He asked me to start at R. I started silently at M, and when I got to R I started speaking out loud.

He asked me to say the alphabet with sounds. I said nothing. He asked me to say the alphabet with the little letters like a, b, c. I said, a, b, c, paused, said d, and then stopped. My stomach sank. I had failed.

He asked me to repeat the sentence he had asked me to remember earlier. I rejoiced – I could pass that one easily.

He asked me about the rhyme that helps you learn to tie your shoelaces. I explained that I learned by watching Dad tie his again and again and again until I could remember the steps. I felt that a story about a rabbit going around a tree was an unnecessary step to achieve getting your shoelaces tied.

My school tie had been the same, thankfully without a silly rabbit story. I had watched my father demonstrate tying a tie until I remembered the steps for myself.

The man asked me to read another sentence, this time silently in my head. I scanned the words at the same speed as my classmates would have read it, and then looked up. He asked me to explain what the words were describing; he said I could read it again if I wanted to.

I looked back down at the words. We both now knew that I

Chapter 29

must have cheated. This was exhausting. He told me to take my time. I studied the words, very conscious that he was waiting. He assured me that there was no rush, which I knew to mean that the man I could not see had a stopwatch and was counting every second.

I explained that it described a sunset in winter.

"How do you know it's winter?"

"Because there's snow on the hills, below the coloured sky."

"What colour is the sky?"

"Red, salmon pink, and orange."

"Is it sunrise or sunset?"

"Sunset."

"How do you know its sunset?"

"In winter the sun rises at nine if we're lucky, and it's never as colourful as the sunset."

I was like the winter sun – never happy getting up, always grey, but glowing at the thought that it was done for a day and rest was coming soon. Or, maybe just pleased it was leaving Scotland to rise in Australia on the other side of the world.

His questions were mixed, like he was trying to derail me or make me forget what I had said moments earlier. His questions came quickly; I would have liked more time to consider my response before delivering it to him, and to the man who was hidden out of my sight.

Do I feel the need to lie to cover for myself? The correct answer would have been wrong, and the wrong answer would also have been wrong. My correct answer versus true answer theory was in jeopardy.

He asked, "Have you ever thought about running away from home?"

Yes, every night at primary school, but I never had the guts to do it. "No, not really."

He asked, "Do you hear voices in your head?" which I recognised as a definite "madness" question. "No," but I did wonder if your own voice counted as a voice and maybe I should have said yes?

The last question was, had I been dishonest in answering any of the other questions? I said that for some questions I would have liked to answer both yes and no.

Three hours of my life gone. The psychiatrist had left to decide my fate: was I stupid and mad with an incurable disease, or just stupid?

Part Three
The Better Years

30

Miss English's classroom was the only one with a wee den tucked in the back. It wasn't soundproof, but it was hidden away from the others. Within that den were two chairs – not school chairs, but rather chairs you could find in someone's living room. They were separated from the class by a bookshelf. I felt safe in there; no one was going to shout at me. It would become safer and more memorable than the special class I went to in primary school. It was in there that I began to understand what Miss English meant when she said that English was not just about reading and spelling.

I now understood that there were stories and information within every book – that no book was just a list of random words broken up by punctuation, although that's how my injured brain read them. I heard these messages far better than I could read them.

One day, Miss English produced a Walkman and a cassette tape. The cassette tape did not hold music, it held someone reading a book: an audio book. A book that I could listen to and follow along in text. I would be able to keep up with our reading homework, so long as the book we were reading in class could also be found on cassette.

Chapter 30

At home, I watched TV with my brother. *Moonlighting, Miami Vice*, I watched what he watched. Years before, we had watched *St Elsewhere*, where Denzel Washington got his big break. The BBC was now showing *Around the World in 80 Days*. I had recently heard the story on a Miss English cassette tape. I had been meant to follow the words in the book, but some stories were more realistic if I just listened, so I did not really follow the words on this book even though I had told Miss English that I had. The rule of lying to tell the truth that was expected remained prevalent. Now, instead of listening to the words, Michael Palin showed me this story in fifty-minute episodes, making its fictional characteristics a reality.

I wondered if this was the imagery I'd missed in nursery rhymes, in all the children's stories I'd never understood. *James and the Giant Peach*, the story was full of flaws. *Little Red Riding Hood*, not even I would be so gullible as to not recognize my own grandmother from a wolf – and how can a wolf talk? *The Wizard of Oz*, yes, let's make friends with a scarecrow, a tin man, and a lion. Everyone wants something, let's all head to the Emerald City, kill a few bad guys, and make everyone feel better about themselves. Why on earth did she not tap her shoes together way at the start if she was that desperate to get home? People said I wasted time dreaming of a better life, but yet it was perfectly acceptable to waste time reading about somebody else's impressions of a dream life.

However, I could imagine Phileas Fogg's world as mine. Michael Palin was showing me that it didn't have to be imaginary; it could be real. I began to no longer dream exclusively of dying but also of travelling, of seeing more than our sleepy town and the one city on the other side of the world. All the people I could meet as I travelled did not need to know my undefined intellectual level. They did not know of my struggle in school. I could be someone else – I could be the fictional character I was developing in my head. Michael Palin brought Phileas Fogg to life; maybe I could bring my own fictional character to life. Maybe there was a yellow brick road for me.

I was lucky, Miss English found all our year's curriculum on audio books. She had lots of audiobooks she thought I might like. She must have had an endless supply, or maybe she wrote the year's curriculum; maybe she did both. I never asked in case it prompted my luck to end.

What was luck? Was luck even real? Hemingway's old man from *Old Man and the Sea* claimed, "Luck is a thing that comes in many forms and who can recognize her?" The old man struggles with the concept of luck, as do I. The old man is unlucky at the start of the story and is unlucky at the end, but there are several ups and downs in between, like the sea. "Bad luck is no way to explain failure." Bad luck was not the reason he had not caught a fish for eighty-four days. Or was it? And if not, what was?

What made him continue to go out fishing while catching nothing, day after day after day? What made him keep going, keep trying, keep ignoring what his village was saying? What made him immune to their judgements? Pride in his former reputation, habit, not knowing what else to do? Bravery? Stupidity? Stubbornness?

Rocky Balboa was the same. How on earth did he have the will to go on, punch after punch after punch? He couldn't even get his hands up to protect himself, falling and staggering to his feet before the count of ten. What gave him the strength to keep going? He did have a supporter in his corner; Mickey looked out for him. I had no Mickey, but I had faced Apollos and Dragos. If I made it out of here, I would run up those steps in Philadelphia, singing "Eye of the Tiger" in my head.

Chapter 30

"But man is not made for defeat, he said. A man can be destroyed but not defeated."

The old man believes in luck but would rather be exact, be skilled, be prepared than to leave things to chance. I could believe the same. He catches his massive fish, his marlin. He won't be defeated by it, would rather die with it – with his brother. He does defeat it, only for it to be stolen from under his nose by the sea vultures and sharks, fuelling his failure, cementing his unluckiness.

He longs for bed. "And bed, he thought. Bed is my friend. Just bed, he thought. Bed will be a great thing. It is easy when you are beaten, he thought. I never knew how easy it was. And what beat you, the thought."

Bed had always been my friend, my safety, my solace. Am I beaten? I was, but am I now? Or am I fighting with my marlin?

The class read *Lord of the Flies*, and I almost trusted that Miss English would not forget that I was not to be selected to read aloud. I followed closely and offered answers to some of her questions so she would know that I was paying attention and didn't just daydream because I had been granted freedom from reading.

Society needs rules, and we all are to obey these rules. If we don't, we would become overwhelmed with self-interest rather than community good and descend into our natural evil. Would this book have been the same if it was a group of girls? Likely, a group of girls would have descended faster than the boys did.

Would society really have stopped functioning if my parents stayed at the hospital beyond the set visiting hours? I doubted it. Like lies, some rules are less important than others for maintaining civilization. When the visiting bell rang, my parents deserted me. The rule could have been ignored, and was ignored by other parents visiting in the hospital ward; it would have caused no one any harm. I decided I would not be ruled by silly rules – I would work out the consequences of breaking or obeying the rule. I would decide. I would not blindly follow without questioning.

I wasn't bad at maths, but once, in the middle of a math class, Miss Maths announced to the class (as if I was stood on the other side of the class, when in fact I was right beside her): "If I'm correcting your spelling, it's a very bad day for you, Rhona Macdonald." Indeed, it was a bad day. I never cried, but I didn't know why I was so upset. I never wanted to be a maths teacher – I never wanted to be any kind teacher – but this incident did secure her a place on my Not To Be Trusted list. Maths also fell onto the list, due to its association with meanness. You can't hide in numbers when the world communicates in words.

"Don't think, sail the course and take what comes."

There is no other option – it's all luck.

31

In *To Kill a Mocking Bird*, Scout's father tries to show that true bravery is to keep fighting, keep persevering, even when you know you are going to lose – that you are going to fail. But, I have to question Atticus Finch, even though he was a clever attorney. Surely to keep fighting against all the odds, when you know the small town's final decision before you even start to present your argument, surely the sensible thing is to give up before you waste your bloody life on it – before you build up other people's hopes, ultimately leading them, in addition to yourself, to disappointment. Why is it cowardly to be realistic?

I met a special dentist when I was twelve years old or so. He was in a different place than the other dentist; he worked from lightly-coloured, sun-kissed, bright rooms. His waiting room had proper children's comics and magazines. I used to look at them, pretending to read – I could read quite fast if I pretended. You just had to look at the word and then look at the next one. No one was going to ask me questions about what I had read, they were going to ask questions about brushing, and teeth, and stuff related to teeth. I was a fast reader in that waiting room.

This dentist had changed his name to orthodontist, and he

was visiting our town. He was a smart young fellow dressed in a pale blue tunic, complete with a full set of shiny white teeth. I wondered if he had been sensible and got the false teeth. There were really posh false teeth now, ones that were not attached to a plate but were rather screwed into your jaw. This was done under a general anaesthetic, so it was possible to get your old "bad" teeth taken out and new, white, straight teeth screwed in all while you were sleeping. To me, this was a great idea. I really wanted those teeth.

He tried to assure me that my mouthful of ulcers was related to my stage of life, and that it would pass. I explained that I'd had ulcers for as long as I could remember, and that every time I brushed my teeth they would bleed. I ate tubes of bonjela – well, I didn't actually eat the tube, but I used lots of its contents every day, trying to protect my ulcers from the teeth that were pushing into them or the tongue that would swipe over them when I was trying to form words to explain how sore my mouth was. He attempted to assure me that it would pass once I got through puberty, and I gave up. There seemed little point in asking what growing a pair of breasts had to do with mouth ulcers.

Someone had decided that I needed braces. Someone had decided that having straight teeth would give me more confidence. I'd heard so much about confidence and how important it was over the years. Confidence was strength, confidence was power, confidence was happiness, but I didn't have any. I wasn't confident. I was weak. I was powerless. I was sad. I was the weak mockingbird. I wondered where everyone else got their confidence from and why had I not got any. Or, perhaps I'd been given my allowance of it then had it stolen away without my noticing.

My father believed I had confidence – he always gave the

Chapter 31

same example when someone suggested I had none. He would say that it took huge amounts of confidence to walk out in front of a roomful of people, from five to five thousand, and complete a set of highland dances without fault. He was the only one who thought this though, so he was wrong. Even I knew he was wrong. Display dancing was not confidence, it was blocking out everyone who was watching you, pretending they're not there, listening to the piper, and remembering the sequence of the steps.

I could grasp seeing the world through others' eyes. I could see how my peers saw me, how teachers saw me, even how my parents saw me through their rose-tinted glasses. I could see my peers – I could see them spell, hear them read. I saw how easy it was for them, how effortless. I could see that I was very different from them, and I knew I would never be like them. Why could I not just give up trying? Why keep banging my head against the wall? I was never going to win. I was the one who had nothing to offer and, worse than a mockingbird, I couldn't even sing. They never bothered to see my life from my shoes; they didn't care. It was a waste of their time.

The orthodontist produced a mouthguard made of metal and explained he was going to fill it with putty, then put one on my top teeth and one on the bottom. I would then have to bite down for a minute, thus allowing the putty to form a print of my teeth. This appeared all quite straightforward. He warned me about the bad taste of the putty – it was not that bad. I bit down at the correct time as requested, but according to him I did not do that properly. So, he decided to help by holding my chin and pressing my head into it.

It's very difficult to scream when someone has a vice grip on your jaw and head and you have two mouth guards and enough plastic putty to choke at least three, but I tried my hardest to scream. The best I could manage was wiggling, which resulted in the vice tightening, so I resorted to giving up – or was it passing out?

The vice slackened, the putty-filled guards removed, and then the bleeding started. I refused to open my mouth to let anything else in. It was only working one way: blood coming out. I got off the chair and headed for the door, a trail of blood and tears connecting the scene to the person. I was told that I had to sit in another chair and calm down. They gave me a comic to read but I could hardly see the pictures, let alone have any interest in the words.

This dentist did what he had done a hundred times before, without any consideration of the facts presented to him. The facts that clearly demonstrated that I was in pain, and that he should stop, but no, he knew best, and he held my mouth closed. The adults know best.

Eventually my mouth stopped pumping out blood, and eventually I let them look in to see what had happened. My gums were torn along the side of my top teeth. He was right: the pain of my ulcers had passed. It had not gone, though, it was just replaced. Once again, just when you think "this is as shit as it can get," you're shown an even shittier level.

It felt like months before I was able to chew with that side of my mouth. My gums were almost healed when my braces arrived, and I had to return to the orthodontist to get them fitted. I was only to have a top brace, and I was not even getting the train track brace. I got this odd one-wire plate brace, but it did not really bother me. It did lead to yet more ulcers, and therefore more pain while eating and brushing. What bothered me more was that on my trips back to see this orthodontist, he would accuse me of not wearing my brace as my teeth were not moving. I had worn the bloody thing. I doubted that he

Chapter 31

had made it correctly; after all, he had surely failed in gaining a mould of my teeth in the manner that is expected. I was not going to correct his mistake though; he would punish me if I did. He was firmly on my Not To Be Trusted list. I accepted his failing and my crooked teeth.

Maybe one day, I could get those flash dentures.

32

When Auntie Nina – the younger of Father's two elder sisters – died in her fifties, she was considered young. Her neighbour found her lying in her kitchen, cold and still. A post-mortem identified a subarachnoid haemorrhage as the cause of death; she was likely dead before her head hit the floor.

Auntie Nina had never married and lived in Viewmount, the family home in Dulnain Bridge, but Father hadn't been there for years. She and my father had been very close, but Nina had pulled away after the introduction of my mother; she considered my mother a little odd, and I got the sense my mother returned a similar feeling. Auntie Nina always visited us, either on Friday afternoons at the workshop or in the evening at the house, where she would stay until at least eleven o'clock at night. Father said it was because she was lonely. She always brought curly kale for Thumper; she had even gone and visited Thumper in the pet shop in Inverness while Father was making his hutch.

When Father entered the family home after Auntie's death, he was shocked. She had turned into a hoarder, with newspapers piled in stacks throughout the house. She had little paths between the boxes, leading from one room to another

Chapter 32

like a rabbit's burrow. She had fallen in the kitchen, one of only two places that was wider than her alleyways. The house had to be tidied and the Will had to be found.

Auntie Grace and Uncle David came from Plymouth with their two adult children, and we each took a room to search to find the Will. Father and Grace were stunned at the current state of the home, and at the discoveries that were uncovered in the week-long tidy up. I learned a lot about my father's story in that week, and in the weeks that followed Auntie Nina's death.

The Macdonald family plot was by the back wall of what was known as the new cemetery, and we visited the spot. Father's parents were already there. I read the stone for Isabella, Father and Nina's mother, who was placed there in May 1942. My father would have been ten years old. William, their father, was buried there in April 1944. I was full of questions but sensed that no one was going to answer them.

The hunt for the Will continued at the house, along with my hunt for answers. I fed the cats, which were hard to count every day. Some days they were five, other days ten. Nina had trays of the best jelly meat you could buy but next to no human food, and what little we discovered was expired. No Will was found, only more questions. A man's belongings were in the bedroom – what man? It was obvious that this man had only just left, so where was he? How long had he lived here? Why had nobody seen/known/met him?

I found photo albums. My grandfather was a carpenter, although he looked like a lawyer in the hand-drawn pencil picture. William the carpenter was twenty-six years his wife's senior. Isabella was his first and only wife.

Papers were found. The man the belongings belonged to was dead. He had been dead for years. He was not local. He had been married and divorced. He was Catholic. The collection of everything had started after his death.

Why had Nina kept him a secret? My father would not have cared if he was Catholic or divorced. His room was the only room not to be filled with boxes. It was a shrine, kept as if he had walked out of it yesterday. His clothes identified his tall and average build. His watch, watch chain, and cufflinks identified him as skilled at something.

I found a letter to Willie and Bella from Tom, congratulating the parents of the "Prince of Viewmount" and stating the motto was correct: "if at first you don't succeed, try, try, try again." I took it to Father. I did not want Grace to see it and hoped that Nina had not seen it either. He read it and declared the motto good. Tom was his uncle – Isabella was known as Bella, and Tom was her brother. He handed it back to me and said I could keep it. I slipped it into my pocket. I would keep it from Auntie Grace; she did not need to know that she and Nina were considered the result of failures.

William the carpenter had stomach cancer when Isabella was diagnosed with breast cancer. At the time, having breast cancer in your late thirties was a death sentence. Auntie Nina looked after both her parents through their illnesses as well as looking after her little brother. Her elder sister had already flown the nest, but Nina battled on. She worked hard at being both nurse and mother. Her mother died in her forties, her father in his seventies, following which Nina was not allowed to look after her brother anymore and Father was sent to live with an aunt in Glasgow who he had never met before.

The Will was finally found, but the information within was not warmly received. The majority of Nina's, and by default the Macdonalds', money was to be donated to an animal rescue, with a small amount going to each of her five nephews and

Chapter 32

nieces. Auntie Grace was outraged and wanted to tear the Will to pieces.

The second part of the Will shattered my father. Nina did not want to lie with her parents in the Macdonald plot – she had already bought a plot in a different cemetery by Alvie church. She had bought a head stone and it was already in place. The Will contained the wording she wanted placed on the stone; all that had to be added was her death date.

We visited the site she had chosen. It was still up against a wall, and beyond the wall lay Loch Alvie. Beside her already-erected stone was an identical stone with identical wording. It was as close as any of us would come to meeting the man she had loved so dearly.

The money was donated to animals and Nina was laid to rest where she wanted to be. The siblings left, hurt and betrayed. If such a hunt had not been undertaken for the Will, Nina would be with her parents and we would never have known that she had felt such love for a man until it was too late to follow her final wishes.

33

On gala day, one side of the pool was jam-packed with spectators. The keen ones sat at the start/finish line and saw the starts and the finishes, but the keen ones also got wet. My mum and dad sat there, my mum with a towel over her knees; she's been to these before. I'd sat on that side when I was younger, watching my brothers. They were fast. They were first. But now I'd left my mum and dad and sat on the other side of the pool with the swimmers. There no room to divide the girls and boys or the different ages, so I sat with my Monday night swimming squad. I sat with my brothers and their friends. I sat with the winners.

Back crawl was always the first race. I was in the youngest age group and girls go before boys, so my back crawl was the first race of the evening. The whole evening, the whole year, would be decided within the next few minutes. We jumped in and the water was crisply cold, oozing through my hair under my hat like an ice cream headache seeping in from the outside. My momentary best friend, who I had gained by losing a few years ago, had been informing everyone who would listen that she would win this first race, and with it break me and win the championship for the group. Every cheer I heard was for her,

Chapter 33

my parents' cheers drowned out – if they were in fact cheering. I never looked. I was going to prove them all very, very wrong. They had all backed the wrong horse.

We settled at the blocks. Take your marks, one deep breath. Get set, pull up on your arm ready for the… She was away, she had launched. Bloody cheater, now I was behind before "go" had even been said. How unfair; how typical. I launched off my block, losing before I'd begun.

The repurposed fire horn blasted and a false start was declared. Thank god. I was furious at the thought she might have got away with such obvious cheating. But this was the first race, and no one was making errors in refereeing yet. Those came later in the evening.

I let another lot of cool water seep through my hair. I was composed, or at least I told myself the lie my head wanted to hear. I could do this. This is what I wanted to do forever. Take your marks, breathe. Get set, pull. GO, explode off the block like a backward dive, a couple of butterfly kicks and back to the surface, and then kick like it's the biggest fight of your life.

The water was cool and calm, the cheers loud then quiet as the water splashed over my face. It did not matter who the cheers were for. Right now, they were all for me. I was swimming in the Olympics. I could see hands at my feet already. I was swimming in the Olympics and winning, stretching strong arm pulls, legs going like hell, steady breathing, already the overhead flags and into the twist and tumble turn. A few butterfly kicks and back to the surface, see the greenest of green ping-pong bats declaring my turn a legal one, no other bats showing yet. The race was mine. The return length was always shorter, unless it was butterfly – then the return length never seemed to end. Overhead flags, a couple of kicks and touch the wall. I had won: Olympic gold. Or at least, first place in the thirteen years girls back crawl, but Olympic gold had a rosier tune to it. It was easy. I won every race that evening and collected my under-thirteen champion trophy with maximum points.

I lay in bed that night, warmed by success but disappointed it would all be forgotten by tomorrow. Tomorrow would be another battle through a school day. I dreamed of being picked by the scout who was in the audience and saw me swim. I always dreamed that the rumour of the scout was true, that they would see my talents and ask my parents to take me to a swimming school far away from everything and everyone I knew. I would train hard and do minimal school work, and years later they would see how great I was. I would win Olympic medals like I had won tonight. I couldn't wait to start.

The weeks passed, and with each day reality sunk in. The scout never came, or if he did he never picked me. But the Glasgow Rangers did win their second league title in a row.

We had another assembly, much the same as any other week, although this one ended in the headmaster stating he was going to call out a list of names, and he wanted those people to stay behind after the assembly. I did not know if this was good or bad, but my name was one of the first to be called – not many names were getting called, so this led me to think we were in trouble. Evan's name was also called though, so at least we could share the blame at home for whatever mischief we had been a part of.

The others filed out and the headmaster explained that each of us had been awarded a prize for our efforts. It was obvious my name had been called in error, but I sat still, hoping to go unnoticed as he went on to explain the prize-giving ceremony. He started to call out the names again and what prize they were to receive. I held my breath. He was going to say "Rhona Macdonald is getting the dunce cap," a prize my peers had

Chapter 33

frequently awarded me. Instead, he said "technical drawing" and moved on to the next person. Technical drawing, what was that? I've got an award, but I wasn't sure what for. Did I even do technical drawing?

I was going to have to find out what this technical drawing was before I got home to inform my parents that someone had actually given me a prize. The four o'clock final bell went and we all walked home. I waited for Evan; he would know what technical drawing was.

"Evan, what's technical drawing?"

"Drawing."

"Drawing art?"

"Drawing drafts for woodwork and metalwork."

"Ah, with the t-bar and french curve and compass?"

"Yes."

"But nothing I make turns out right."

"So you can't make the stuff, but you can draw the stuff."

"Drawing is easy."

"That's why you got the prize."

I announced my prize at home and my parents seemed very pleased. They said they would be there for the prize-giving. I knew they would be there; Evan was collecting prizes in physics and math after all.

I did have to question this technical drawing prize. Was it a real subject? Was it not linked to woodwork and metalwork, both of which I was far from average at? I guess not. Woodwork was hard, I did not like the noise or smell of metalwork, and none of my plans ever worked out. As for the plans, were these not the plans the teacher would explain as he drew most of it on the board, and then ask us to draw it after he had rubbed it out? It's not technical drawing, it's watching someone else do something and copying it. It's simple memory work, no different from any other class. But hey, if they really wanted to give me a prize, fine. I'd have it. I put my unanswered question to the back of my mind.

"Don't think, sail the course and take what comes"

Our parents were indeed there at prize-giving, clapping for everyone as they collected their awards. They never clapped for me though, but then I felt a bit better as they never clapped for Evan either.

They were talking with the headmaster afterwards, and I walked up to them to hear the headmaster saying, "...he has the best maths mind this school has even seen, there is nothing more the maths department is able to teach him."

Then he saw me. "And here's another clever soul, you must be very proud." Liar – onto the Not To Be Trusted list for him. I smiled as my parents both answered, "We are."

Why do people constantly lie to me?

The summer after Secondary One, we replaced the caravan with a plane and flew to Spain. I was on my first airplane flight; we were all on our first airplane flight. Father was not encouraged by the fact they played "Knocking on Heaven's Door" as we slowly climbed through the dark clouds of Glasgow. The music did not bother or upset me – I was not listening to it. Instead, I was listening to power of the engines, which were not like Isle of Man TT engines, nor like Silver Shadow Rolls Royce engines. These engines were like the RAF training flights that roared over our small town. These were real engines with real power, and they lead to real escape. They took you through the clouds, so they took you through heaven.

Fancy Marbella was our first destination. We stayed at Puerto Banús, the flashiest marina on the Costa del Sol, where the filthy rich and not even that famous parked their luxury yachts. Father spent most of the week wandering round and round

Chapter 33

and round in awe of their lavish lifestyles – it even gave new meaning to his saying of "how the other half live."

My brothers and Calum's girlfriend took me to clubs. The bouncers did not care that I was thirteen, although they did care that my brother was wearing jeans one night and flip-flops another. I discovered by a process of elimination that Calum's Johnnie Walker and lemonade was a perfectly acceptable alternative to orange juice. I was thirteen, pretending I was eighteen. If I was really eighteen then I wouldn't have to go back to school. It was nice being in the alcohol-filled eighteen-year-old's world.

Next, we travelled to the British Gibraltar and looked out over the strait. We then moved up the coast a little and took a trip to the truly breath-taking Ronda. People say Scotland is breath-taking, but those people need to go to Ronda's New Bridge, which isn't that new and took forty-plus years to build. Or, they need to see the view from the New Bridge. We then moved to Fuengirola before returning to rainy, damp, cold Glasgow. I don't think Father had ever been so pleased to be in the dark and wet city, as his enthusiasm for the overseas had dwindled the longer the holiday went on. Mine, however, had grown.

I was more determined than ever to leave our sleepy little town and travel the world. I willed myself to be eighteen faster so I could be done with school and off again, soaring above the clouds.

34

The next school year, English started off with F. Scott Fitzgerald's *The Great Gatsby*. As usual, Miss English had this on cassette tape for me. There were even films, and our first classes on this book solely involved watching them.

"You can't repeat the past, but of course you can," Gatsby said as the lights turned off and the fountain stopped. I fell in love with the dazzling blues eyes of Robert Redford. The art deco glamour. The champagne. The Charleston dance, wonderfully coordinated to the soulful rhythm of jazz, scored higher in my mind than Torvill and Dean's "Boléro." I decided that I would have to go to America as none of this would ever happen in our unconscious town.

I would chase the dream and I would gamble on the betrayal, the shattered American dream. What was one more failure on my list of failures?

I asked Evan if he had any jazz music. He gave me The Best of Nina Simone.

"Fitzgerald based this novel on his reality, on his life experiences. Does anyone know any other American writers to have this trend?" Miss English asked.

Hemingway joined the First World War as a volunteer first

Chapter 34

aider and was then injured at the front line. *A Farewell to Arms* is about an American first aider who is injured at the front line. But Miss English did not tell me if Hemingway was an old fisherman who had not caught anything for eighty-four days when she gave me that cassette tape, so I kept my suggestion to myself.

Later, behind the bookcase in the comfy chairs, I offered Miss English my answer, which she said was correct. On discussion, it turned out that Hemingway *was* a fisherman and did catch marlin off the Florida coast. I should really go to America.

Hemingway was sixty-one years old when he died, so not really an old man at sea, but there were links between him and his writing. Frances Scott Fitzgerald was only forty-four when he died after a heart attack. Both men drank too much. Fitzgerald had died before *The Great Gatsby* was considered great. He had other books which were not considered greats, so he may or may not have died feeling like a failure.

These two men shared more than their American-ness and taste for alcohol. They knew each other from when they had both lived in Paris. Fitzgerald had helped Hemingway edit his first novel, *The Sun Also Rises*. Miss English could get me the cassette of that book, if I wanted.

I did.

35

Technical drawing was now my favourite subject, and I tried exceedingly hard to be good at it and put in a huge amount of concentration. Technical drawing might be the subject that I'm good at in the same way as Evan is with maths. Distressingly, the person who sat beside me did not like technical drawing and did not like me or the fact that I liked it and was good at it. She insisted on hitting my elbow several times during each class, ensuring that my drawing looked similar to hers. This was my subject, and she was ruining it for me. I hit her on the head with my pencil case one class after forewarning her several times what the outcome would be if she did not stop. She screamed like I had stabbed her, which was followed by the teacher shouting at me. I was going to have a find a new favourite subject. I silently added her to my list.

    I was awkward at most sports. Dancing had given me strong legs and swimming kept me toned, but when given any type of racket or bat combined with a fast-approaching ball, I found my almost ten-stone weight too cumbersome to get my arm to extend. In addition, my eyes preferred not to watch and automatically closed in preparation for the impact – depending on who had just fired it at me, it would strike with different

Chapter 35

weights and different levels of pain. I fared a little better at basketball and netball as my weight was an advantage, making me hard to push over.

In winter we skied cross-country, and I loved it. I liked being out with the cold biting at your cheeks, your body warmth dependant on your speed. I loved being first, or at least right up with the teacher who usually took on the leader role. I hated waiting for the others – the last ones always looked cold and miserable, like they were in actual pain. They looked like I may have looked in the classroom.

This winter also brought another family trial. I was out one evening building snowmen and attempted igloos when my eldest brother's girlfriend passed by with her dog. I threw one snowball at her; she did not throw any back and kept walking. Somehow, however, she returned to her home ten minutes later covered in snow.

The court was held in the dining room. I had apparently chased her down the road throwing snowballs at her. I stated again and again that I had thrown just one and she had walked off. I did not throw any more. I did not chase her down the road.

I was a known liar to the jury I faced and she was older, she knew better. She said I chased her down the road throwing snowballs, so that is what the jury believed. Why would she lie? It did not matter what I said. I again repeated the truth, but their decision was made.

Her lies made me look like a liar, and on this occasion I was not. She used her age and her power to turn my own blood and bone against me. I would never trust her. I did not need her in my life. She was added to the list.

At school we canoed in summer, graduating from the swimming pool to the river. We would paddle down the fastest-flowing river in Scotland in small groups, annoying the fishermen who had paid vast sums of money to stand in freezing cold water and drink from their hip flasks. I found it quite relaxing. I'm sure the clever kids the teacher spent most of the day shouting at did not find it as relaxing, but the fact that the shouting was not directed at me was extremely tranquil. Besides, they deserved to be shouted at, and it was satisfying to see them receive a little of what they sorely deserved.

The rapids did not really concern me. The washing machine did not live up to its reputation, but then again, the people that came through the washing machine on spin cycle would likely not have agreed with me.

During a lunch break, the PE teacher came up and sat down beside me and quietly asked if sometimes I got confused between my right and left hands. I said no. She said that she was telling me to paddle with my right and I kept using my left, so I changed my answer to yes, sometimes. I said that when she was saying right repeatedly, I thought she meant to paddle again and again with the right. I never thought I was doing anything wrong. She said I was lucky not to have capsized and asked what she should say or do so that I could recognize my error sooner. I said that most people just keep shouting at me until I figure it out. She said she could call out the hand I needed to paddle with, and if I was using the wrong one she would call out "the other one" rather than the repeated right or left instruction.

I quite liked Miss PE. She was also my swimming teacher, and I could do well in her subjects. She did shout at lot at the kids who did not fare so well, which was a little unnerving, but I told myself that she wasn't shouting at me. I could swim and almost canoe.

The roll training took a little to get used to; it seemed silly to

Chapter 35

actively turn your canoe upside down. The water was always freezing and instantly bit hard as it ran down your life vest and through your hair, but all one had to do was relax. It was a simple drill: tap on the bottom of the canoe and wait for another canoe end to touch so you could pull round, as simple as a bath duck held under the water will pop round to sit proudly on his bottom at the surface. The paddle rolls got better, and soon we were doing head rolls. This canoeing was all well and good, but what possible benefit did it have? How was this going to get me get a job and me out of my hometown?

Miss English also got me *Death in the Afternoon*. I did not enjoy this novel, but I did find it intriguing. There was an art form to the cruel sport of bullfighting, and the stadium my family and I had visited in Ronda was impressive. Hemingway's passion is infectious and his confusion understandable, but I did not share Hemingway's enthusiasm for torturing an animal and making it suffer. I was a supporter of the bull, so hypothetically if I would go and see the street carnival of the Bull Run in Pamplona, I'd tell myself the bulls were running for their freedom, not to the stadium where their death awaited. Neither were on my To Do list, though.

At the end of my second year in Grammar school, it came time to choose my specialist subjects. These subjects would form the path toward your future career, something I'd never really thought about. I was always too occupied with surviving the year, or month, or day, or even just the next five minutes. A career was supposed to be something that would enable me to financially support myself and follow my dreams. What were my dreams? To survive long enough to escape. So what was my chosen career? I had no idea.

I needed to think of a future career. Needed to think of a

future; about the possibility of surviving school and having a future. I didn't want to hope too much.

I found it immensely difficult to answer the question, "Well, what are you interested in?" After seeing the advertisements by the World Wildlife Federation, I wanted to help animals. I was interested in stopping animal testing and in catching, tagging, and releasing big cats in Africa. I was interested in making my mother's dinner menus difficult by becoming vegetarian. I was interested in swimming for Scotland and having everyone cheer for me. I was interested in running away and re-inventing myself. I was interested in being Michael Palin's cameraman, getting to see all the great sights that he saw. I wasn't interested in fitting in any longer. It was too late to fit in – I didn't belong here. I wanted to leave, and I wanted to work with animals.

My mind still had a life of its own.

Everyone said that choosing my subjects was the most important thing in my life. Was everyone correct? This was the same everyone who said the school years were the best years of your life. This "everyone" were liars. They talked shit.

After weeks of deliberating, I said I was interested in travelling and in working in animal welfare and protection. Mere seconds later, my career advisor told me that I wasn't clever enough to go to veterinary school. I wouldn't be accepted, and without being a vet I wouldn't be able to work in animal protection. It was time to stop dreaming.

She suggested the police, and I thought about it. Dad said that police have few friends, and the only friends they do have are other police. That they were boring and disliked by the community even though they were needed. That they worked hard for their community and never received the thanks or acknowledgement that they both earned and deserved. I did not want to join the police.

Chapter 35

Becoming a chef was another suggestion. I did like food – I ate every day. I liked cook books that listed ingredients I'd never heard of and could never find in our little corner shop of a supermarket. I would need to study French if I wanted to be a chef, though. French, I was told, was the language of the kitchen. I found French hard. Mr French used to put bits of blackboard chalk on a table and smash it into dust with an old leather belt that my father used to get beaten with at school. His class was never one to lose concentration in. I was looking forward to not sitting in that class. I was not convinced I wanted to be a chef, but I was certain I wanted to find where the ingredients came from. I wanted to go and taste all the different foods in their native countries.

I thought about marriage and children – the "normal" thing to do, although it seemed alien to me. I did not want to become a parent, to have the same job as my mother. I would not be responsible for bringing another human being into this fight we call life.

The next suggestions were a being travel agent or an air hostess. I was unconvinced that travel agents actually got to go anywhere; rather, they spent their day booking the holiday of a lifetime for other people. I did not think I needed that daily kick in the face. Was being a travel agent even considered a career?

Air hostessing I did not dismiss instantly, even though it would put me back in the French class as well as German. I was concerned about the expected level of prettiness, as well as my struggle with French. My father called the profession being "a waitress in the sky," but they talk about oxygen masks falling, emergency landings, life jackets, exit lighting, things that could save you or kill you. Sure, they may give out meals and collect trays, but when and if the big bird is falling from the sky, I doubt they would be checking their makeup. Father thought I'd do better to aim for being the pilot. That was an utterly useless suggestion – I think a pilot would know which side was left without holding a fucking imaginary pen. I dismissed both options.

Time was up: I had to pick the subjects that would decide the rest of my life. I picked subjects that I liked and teachers that I liked.

English and maths were core, as too were a language and a science.

I stayed clear of physics. Evan had set a high standard for that one, and I was going to try and not be a complete idiot in every one of my chosen subjects. There was no physics teacher at the time too, and what if Miss Fucking Primary Six turned up with her wicked smile and a degree in teaching physics? I wasn't risking that.

I almost chose chemistry, which I actually enjoyed, but the teacher was unpredictable and could easily flare into an unexplained rage. I thought it best to stay clear of her. Calum had taken chemistry and although his stories were funny, I was unconvinced she was ready to teach another Macdonald, especially one that was so different.

Biology was the most animal-like of the sciences and although I had been advised not to aim to work with animals, it was the only science left. Again, there was an unpredictable teacher, complete with a wonky eye; when he flew into a rage, everyone was unsure at who his anger was addressed, maybe even him. Neither eye had ever focused on me during any of his rages, though, so I would try and continue that luck.

I couldn't wait to depart the French class. Calum had claimed he was an only child and therefore did not have to explain about his younger brother and sister and their ages and their

Chapter 35

like and dislikes. He said did not have any pets either. This had worked well for him. He did two years of French and then dropped it just as Evan entered the same classroom and said that he had one older brother called Calum and one younger sister. Evan was good at French, so then I entered the same classroom and proved not to be very good at French nor very clever at avoiding the questions. It was also claimed that I had developed a crush on a boy who happened to be the French teacher's son, which both the son and father found out about. So it was au revoir to French, although I did it with concern as a few of my possible careers "required" French.

I still had to pick a language, so German it was. I was okay at German. I thought a lot of the words sounded like English words, and providing I could remember the English word I could usually get to the expected German word. This was not the way we were taught; we were taught that the sounds were the key. Life had taught me sounds were only the key to confusion, and that it was better not to make the same mistake twice. I learned the required German phrases by association to random English words. *Ich harbour woof jara cult*: I am twelve years old. *Ich harbour swine brooder unt nina hunt:* I have two brothers and a dog

The next choice was between history, geography, and modern studies. I liked all three, and I was almost okay at all three. I was never first, second, or third in any test, but I'd not be named and shamed in the last or second-to-last rankings either. They were safe subjects. The teachers, however, were not so safe. I chose geography as it had the most placid teacher out of the three.

The next two groups were an odd bunch made up of PE, tech drawing, art and design, and a few others.

I enjoyed art and design. I could draw, but I would have to

learn how to critique work. It was the key to an architectural career. I'd received my prize in tech drawing, but after the pencil case incident I could not trust the teacher not to turn against me.

Home economics was an easy choice. I really liked the teacher, and the subject was one of few that I could see the value in. I could understand that one day it would be useful to know about consumer needs and rights. Hell, maybe one day I'd need to know what the essentials were for a newborn baby and why a good-fitting mattress is important for a crib or cot, although I doubted it. But people told me I'd change my mind, and that one day I would be a loving and giving mother like my own. I was more interested in how to change a plug and what all the little triangles on electrical goods meant. Home ec was picked.

So, my subjects were English, math, biology, German, geography, art and design and home economics. I had no career planned, just a shattered dream of helping conserve animals in Africa.

It was the end of another year. Mark Hateley almost single-handedly secured the third championship in a row for the Glasgow Rangers by scoring two goals in the final match of the season. There was another swimming championship won with maximum points. There was even another school prize – home economics. Evan was awarded dux. Our parents attended the prize-giving and clapped for neither of us.

Evan was leaving. He had long since survived primary school. In secondary school he had liked his physics teacher, Frank Saunders. Saunders had opened up a new and interesting world that Evan could easily understand. Sadly, Mr Physics lost his life to cancer while Evan was still under his tutelage, but Evan continued to learn to the point that

Chapter 35

there was nothing more the maths department could teach him.

Evan was going to attend Warwick University and read *Pure Mathematics*, but first he was going to backpack around Australia. My ally was leaving me behind.

36

Miss English also left me. She was teaching the bottom class; I had made it into the top class and would be taught by Mr English. In the safe seat behind the bookcase, Miss English tried to assure me that Mr English would teach me the same as she had. There would be no reading aloud and no surprise questions. She could and would get the audiobooks that he was going to use in the year, as she knew what books he would teach.

There was a library of audiobooks – not in our crappy school, but Miss English was well-connected. My father might be correct. It's not what you know, it's who you know.

Miss English was definitely correct: Mr English never questioned me or asked me to read aloud, but his class was noisy – especially the Woebetide boy. He ran wild like sepsis, infecting those around him. He was the same in Maths. Mr Math, who was actually Dr Math, was called nothing but "nurse" in the whinnying, whimpering voice of the Woebetide boy. Dr Math snapped several times and completely lost all self-control, and he often had to leave the class. Why did the teacher leave? Miss English sent the Woebetide boy, or anyone who didn't want to learn, out of the room – he would

Chapter 36

not prevent those that did want to learn from learning in her class. He was the same in geography. Mr Geography hid in his cupboard for at least part of our lesson, which just added to the ripple for rumours that he was drinking in there. Who could blame him? This kid was a nightmare. Sadly, I realized that just as I had picked subjects with placid teachers, the Woebetide boy had done the same as he knew he would be able to distract the class constantly.

Home ec and art and design were good. During those periods, the Woebetide boy was busy blowing up the chemistry lab and perfecting his smarty-pants replies in French.

The Glasgow Rangers won their fourth title in a row.

In the lead up to the annual swimming gala, I was asked if I would take part in a demonstration of different canoe rolls, with and without the paddles. Sure, I could do that, as well as swim. I felt "confidence" in winning swimming, despite having no confidence and everyone trying to aid me in finding more. But, I was flattered to be asked. I'd always enjoyed canoeing, although I was more just grateful for not being terrible at it. The teacher never screamed at me, though she was reported to have a wicked temper. She apparently screamed at some other kid that his father was spineless; the child in question's father was not handicapped at all, he was a respectable and admired local businessman. She could scream anything she liked, though, so long as she ran out of screaming before she saw me.

I had to do a few lunchtime training sessions to figure out the routine, but it all seemed simple enough. Even though this school was big enough to hide in, it was always a relief to be involved in lunchtime activities. If I was lucky, someone might even ask what I was planning to do during the impending lunch hour, or whether I wanted to walk down to the high street in their group for a sandwich. I'd proudly say "Thanks, but I can't. I'm in the pool."

During one training session, I was perfecting my head roll. My canoe was almost sitting correctly upright, my head coming out of the water last, and as I was about to take a breath of air, my canoe and I were unexpectedly looking at the black lines on the bottom of the pool. I was confused as to what had just happened. I could have accepted this occurrence as being possible on the river, but it did not make sense in the swimming pool.

Again I rolled, and again I did not clear the water line, although I was sure I should have. I got a mouthful of chlorinated water and was looking at the black lines once more. I rolled again and got air, but then was again faced with the black lines. Those lines had been friendly to me in the past, but right now I knew I could not stay in their company.

How could I just forget how to roll when I had done it hundreds of times? How do you lose a skill so completely right when you need it most? This had happened before – I'd forget where I'd been when questioned about why I was late or covered in mud, and I always forgot how to read when asked to do just that. Why did I forget so much? Or rather, why did I forget the bits of my memory that I needed at that given moment?

I saw feet standing by the black line. They looked like twisted feet, but water can distort images. I hit the bottom of the canoe but the feet did not move, were not offering any sort of help. I rolled and gained a mixture of air and chlorine water and finished again looking at the black lines. I rolled again but this time the canoe didn't move; it had turned into concrete. Another roll and nothing – was I set in this concrete? The feet were still there. Again another roll, again another mix of chlorine and air. I hammered the bottom with the last of my

Chapter 36

strength, but those feet stood as if they too were cemented in place. They were not going to help.

I flipped the spray deck and began to depart company with my canoe, which now began to move. It was rolling itself, rolling in the opposite direction to my unconsciously chosen side to exit, the hard plastic edge scraping down my leg from mid-thigh to foot while digging deep into my knee and ankle. I was upright, feet on the pool floor, head in the air, retching, coughing, splattering, gasping in more air than was required to sustain life. I could hear laughing. I looked around. The owner of the deformed feet that would not move was laughing. I half swam, half pulled myself along the wall and up the pool steps. The owner of the feet, no longer laughing but shouting, demanded my return to empty the canoe that was now upside-down, full of water and without me as an attachment. It was my responsibility to get it out of the water and tie it up on the wall.

"Fuck you" was my only response.

I headed for the change room, where my body happily continued to exchange water for air. I would not have to worry about what canoeing job opportunities lay ahead; I would never sit in another canoe.

I was asked what happened, what made me change my mind about doing the demonstration, but I could not confess to nearly drowning. No one would believe me anyway. Rhona drowning was as unlikely as Rhona being clever. I went with "I want to concentrate on my swimming on the night" and kept my leg concealed under tights for the week.

I pondered why had I been so cross with him holding my canoe. I was not expected to drown, was I? If I had, then he would have got the blame – he would have been responsible for giving me the one thing that I longed for so long. Why had I struggled? Why did I not just relax with the black lines? Why had I responded to my body's demand for air? I had been offered a way out, and in reply I'd said "fuck you."

A week later at the gala, my leg still showed the bruise that ran almost its length and the skin on the side of my knee and ankle had not completely healed, but the black lines were once again friendly. I won my age group with maximum points. The canoe demonstration was done by two boys, one of whom had been my canoe holder. There was no need for my parents to attend the prize-giving.

37

As I entered into my teenage years, I saw a different person when I looked in the mirror. The person who looked back at me was not a cry baby with mousy brown hair cut into the same style as her brothers. The person who looked back could have red hair or blonde hair, had grown breasts, had well-shaped legs, had developed a thick outer shell to protect herself that was getting stronger every day.

A boy had taken my school bag earlier in the year and felt the need to go through my belongings, which included sanitary products. This event coincided with a very annoying song lyric being sung at me, one which accompanied advertising for Tampax on the television. Every time I saw him or one of his friends, there would be a chorus of "It's my life." I ignored it for weeks before I took action.

I told Mrs Math, the registration teacher; I had already witnessed her fast and loud temper. Lunchtime registration was over and we were moving out to our first afternoon class when she asked the singer to wait behind. I hovered round the corner and just as I had hoped, she laid into him with both barrels. I left them to it and moved on to class, hoping that this would make things better rather than worse.

Someone asked me, why had I told Mrs Math and not Miss English? I simply said that Mrs Math was our registration teacher while Miss English was our English teacher, and it was not an English problem. She seemed content with my answer. What I had really done was select a teacher that I had justification to tell – essentially, any teacher that taught me – but more importantly chosen the one who had the wildest temper.

The bag thief and searcher caught me by the arm during the afternoon.

"You retarded bitch."

"Pardon?"

"Fucking retarded bitch."

"Oh, Mrs Math spoke with you."

"You'll be sorry you did that."

"I have to report back to her and let her know how things are going on the music front, so if I were you, I'd pick a different target. Excuse me."

Who said lying was bad? I never had to report back to Mrs Math. I never heard the song sang at me again, and when I saw the ad I was now warmed by my victory.

I still felt like the same miserable hopeless failure, but at least I did not look the same miserable hopeless failure.

Miss English was my teacher again – another victory. I was still in the top English class, but Miss English and Mr English had swapped.

Animal Farm was first book for the year. The class took turns to read, and I was mercifully still not being selected. We discussed the novel as a class, and I found it challenging to understand and frustratingly difficult to explain. I was quiet for much of the discussion – on this occasion, it was not because I feared my answer was incorrect, but merely because I did not have an answer.

Chapter 37

When Miss English asked me about my thoughts, I had to say that I didn't know, that I didn't like it, reverting to my stupid baby language.

I found the book unrealistic, fantastical even. Two pigs teaching animals to read and write, squabbling over powers, standing, making other animals' lives a misery, backstabbing and blaming others, the less equal now too brainwashed or frightened to fight, deciding surrender is the easier option. Unnervingly, this unrealistic story was too uncomfortably resonant with my primary years. I didn't like animal abuse. I don't like hidden stories – it takes my brain too long to find the story within words. There's no need to hide meaning under a double layer. If this story was about Stalin's Soviet Union and the Russian Revolution, then let's discuss the facts. Let's leave the poor horse alone and get it in the correct classroom: history.

I felt the same way about Orwell's *Down and Out in Paris and London*, which Miss English had leant me as extra reading. The story had been previously rejected as an outright lie, someone pretending to be something they weren't. Why would someone successful – or, if not classed successful, someone who had supportive family and could have been in employment – choose to leave a job and act poor? I was fairly certain there were plenty of people labouring in Parisian restaurants, and I'd seen the homeless in London. Let them write something, support them, give them a chance – let them tell the true story. Orwell stole the poor Parisian and Londoner's story.

I confirmed with Miss English that *Animal Farm* was written by the same Orwell as *Down and Out in Paris and London*, and mentally marked him as a dangerous, cunning liar, someone best to be avoided. He was added to the list.

Orwell was not the only writer to do this to me, and it wasn't just novels that I could get confused by. *At Grass* was read and dissected – I never saw or heard of retired race horses. But at least it only took one lesson before Philip Larkin joined George Orwell. Why double hidden meanings within literature was deemed exceptional, I did not understand.

I asked Miss English if Orwell knew Hemingway or Fitzgerald. Hemingway had met Orwell, although seemingly they met only once and they were not friends. I didn't have to ask – I knew George Orwell was not dyslexic.

A third victory came this year in the form of dance. The visitors that overran our town loved a ceilidh and loved highland dancing, whether it was a solo sword dance or intertwined broadswords. My favourite was always the Strathspey Reel of Tulloch. Following one of these displays, my parents were approached by an awards officer for the Duke of Edinburgh Award Scheme who was helping set up and implicate the Award Scheme in Belgium, known as the Benelux Award Program. A ceilidh was planned to formally promote the Awards Scheme and would be attended by the Princess of Ligne – who was the sister of the Grand Prince of Luxemburg – and members of the education authority from throughout Belgium, and they needed a highland dancer. My parents were asked if I could and would travel to Brussels to do a demonstration of highland dancing at the ceilidh, and they in turn asked me. I was to be the only dancer – the younger girls weren't asked. I was in need of a career, so yes, I would and could certainly do this.

I travelled to Brussels by overnight bus and ferry and stayed with a local family. Our only common language was pointing, but we got on well.

The main ceilidh was held in the Civic Centre in Belgium. I was on stage and everyone within the hall was watching, waiting. The house lights went down, and soon the audience was hidden behind the dazzling spotlights. The piper started

Chapter 37

and I followed, dancing as if to myself with just the piper as witness to my performance. It was quiet, without the usual shouts and cheers that would come in a Scottish ceilidh. I finished, I bowed, my lights went out and the audience's came back. I glanced around, and everyone seemed to be clapping. I was halfway through with the Highland Fling, Seann Truibhas, Hielan Laddie and Barracks Johnnie successfully completed, and I walked off stage to change.

I returned for my second half after the guests had finished eating their mains. Again, their lights went out and the spotlights were on me; again, it was peaceful. I started this section with one of my favourites – Flora MacDoanld's Fancy – then Blue Bonnet's Over the Border, then Scottish Lilt, and then completed the performance with Scots Measure. I enjoyed this second set more, although I'm not entirely sure why. Maybe it was because this last set was less rigid than the first. The dances felt more graceful, easier to cover any error or at least to get past the halfway point without mishaps. Again, the lights swapped over and everyone I saw was clapping. I curtsied and followed my piper offstage, where I met a row of people as they passed me in line. Some were the Royals, but I did not recognise any – none of these people had been guests of the British Royal family at any of the Braemar Gatherings that I had been to. I was a bit too puffed after dancing to engage in much conversation, so they said I dance beautifully and then quite quickly moved on to the piper.

After this I performed at several halls and schools. None of them cause me anxiety. I knew my steps, I had not chosen complicated dances, and there was no one judging my performance. After four days, I returned to Grantown by bus and ferry. I kept the front page of the Badnoch and Strathspey Herald that explained this story alongside the paper with my "best local dancer" story. I was doubly prepared to answer any questions about my dancing abilities. The younger girls had even quit their parades round the school classes with their cups and trophies.

Could I make a career of dancing? I did not know. But if I could, at least I probably wouldn't need to learn French.

38

Work experience fortnight arrived, the two weeks where you work alongside real people in the community doing real work. The only problem was that I still had no career planned. So, I ended up in one of the many old folks' homes for my work experience.

The building had once been a grand hotel, possibly the grandest of the town, but due to the lack of guests its role had changed. The place was once again full, but now of people waiting to die. Families paid vast amounts of money for their much-loved parents to live in these places with a few items that they or their families had selected to surround them, constantly reminding them of the life they once had. Family homes were sold to fund the pain.

The inside was always warm in temperature but still felt very cold to me. Every day was the same. I would help the health care assistants wash, dress, and move the in-patients from their room to another room that had music or a TV disrupting the silence. Many of the men had faded, blurry-edged tattoos. I asked some what they were, what they represented, but they never answered; some would look at the mark on their arm but never comment. Then one day, a man gave me an answer:

"A better time." I returned his response with a weak smile, the strongest I could manage, and I never asked the meaning of any tattoo ever again. The one answer I had was likely the correct and truthful answer for all the different tattoos on all the different arms.

The residents all looked the same, faces a web of wrinkles, the life sucked out of them. If you looked at the row of feet, you saw they all wore one of three different styles of slippers. These people were all identical, waiting for the same identical end. They would numbingly sit in the dayroom until it was time to prepare for the next activity. Few visitors came, likely only the most loyal. Maybe more visitors came on the weekends or after working during the day. Or, maybe it was easier not to visit at all, not to see what had become of the once much-loved family member; maybe it was easier to remember them as they were before. But how did turning away help these people in these chairs? They were still alive, albeit just. Could they not still be loved? It looked like the answer was no, so they sat in the dayroom and waited for whatever came next. Every "next" began and finished with the same toilet/wash/change routine, like a one-year old.

The activity I hated most was eating/feeding in the dining room. People like me slowly guided spoonfuls of watery scrambled eggs into mouths. Tongues as long as a hot, happy dog's reached out to meet the spoon of cold yellow mush. Teeth that were ill fitting often dropped out; some were placed on the tabletop beside the decorative salt and pepper shakers. The in-patients gummed the eggs with their tongue and mouth's roof, sucking their overly milky tea through the straw of a child's non-spill beaker, the eggs rolling down the straw into the tea when they stopped for breath. The tea-egg mixture escaped out of corners of their post-stroke mouths into bibs, some of

Chapter 38

which were plastic and had an upturned collection pouch at the bottom. Was this as bad as their lives would get?

I tried not to look at the collection within the pouch and prayed that their hands would not go investigating its contents – some liked the differing textures that could be found inside. If they did, I'd slowly remove their hand and wipe it with a damp face cloth, hoping that they would not return the hand into the pouch. Other feeders caught the mixture as it ran down the resident's face and neck and spooned it back into a mouth for attempt number two or three. There was no conversation; everyone sat in silence. Were they, like me, concentrating hard on not vomiting?

It was all sickening. The patients' silence expressed their disgust. The few that spoke recalled stories of the sirens, of collecting their children to head to the safety of the bomb shelters. I rather liked these stories and would listen intently, but the stories never changed – they were just repeated and repeated and repeated.

It was during these two weeks that I saw my first dead body, a lucky in-patient who fulfilled their dream of going to sleep and never waking up. They were found cold in the morning by a health care assistant and a schoolgirl, one of whom screamed and rushed out of the room, the other who stayed and stroked the old lady's grey hair, recalling her own childhood dream. And within those two weeks, my second death arrived: an old fellow who drifted off into a never-ending afternoon snooze while basking in the sun, as happy as a cat sunbathing.

There was peace in that place, but you had to wait for it. By comparison, a vet would help old animals who were unable to look after themselves out of their pain. He would not be spoon-feeding them as they sat in their own shit; he would take the dream to the animal. Animals did not have to suffer, they did not have to wait for death, but humans did.

Rhona Macdonald

I was there for two weeks, and my work experience showed me that I never wanted to work or live in an old folks' home.

39

The school bell rang, indicating it was time to change subjects. I was going to my favourite class, and my favourite teacher. But Miss English was not in her classroom, and some other woman was sat in her chair. No one had warned me of an impending change; I wasn't prepared. My mind gathered momentum as this new person explained that Miss English was sick, and that she was the stand-in English teacher. My mind raced faster and faster and I had to fight to keep my edges in, fight to stay upright.

What was wrong with Miss English? How long was she going to be sick for? What if she had cancer, like Mr Physics? She might die. My mind was out of control. I had fallen. I was sat on the back of my skis, hurtling down the slope toward failure once again. Miss English may never teach me again. What would happen to me? How selfish am I? Miss English has cancer and is going to die, and I'm wondering who'll be on my side at school. I am a terrible person.

Miss Stand-in English asked someone to start reading. Oh God, she was asking people to read out loud. She didn't know that I don't get chosen for this task. We had been in the midst of Shakespeare's *Julius Caesar*. Oh my fucking God. She was selecting people to read *Julius Caesar*. I couldn't do this. Even if I declined to read, or said I don't read, I'd be admitting to my classmates what they all had never noticed.

I couldn't read *Julius Caesar*, not out loud. It wasn't even normal English, it was Old English. You had to flick to the glossary at the back to understand what it meant. I tried to read ahead so as to be best prepared for the humiliation, but I couldn't see the words as water was clouding my vision. I couldn't do this. I'm not doing this. I whispered to my neighbour, the girl who read books by torchlight under her bedding and who couldn't swim very well, that I felt sick, which was actually true. I pushed my chair away from my desk, stood up, and walked out of the class. When I closed the door, I ran along the empty corridor, down the steps and into the toilet where I hid until the bell sounded again.

I was relieved to hear Miss English didn't have cancer and was not going to die. She would be back to teaching the following week. I just had to survive this week.

Miss Stand-In English's second lesson was a spelling test. Fucking brilliant!

Fifty words. She said them, and we had to write them down. I calmed my mind and assured myself that Miss English would be marking this test and would forgive me for missing most of the fifty that I'd attempted.

I had my paper carefully guarded so no eyes could see my blank spaces filled by a collection of random letters I put there to trick Miss Stand-In English into thinking that I was answering. I was ready to hand it in for eventual marking when Miss Stand-In English asked us to pass our paper to the right. My brain panicked. I gripped my paper tightly, unwilling to share its contents. I was going to have to walk out again. My alphabetically linked, non-swimmer, reader-under-the-sheets

Chapter 39

neighbour reached out her hand and gripped the corner of my paper. She whispered, "Don't worry, you have passed." I let go.

The next minutes passed with an air of hazy surrealism. My neighbour proceeded to mark my incorrect answers correct.

Miss Stand-in English called a number and wanted a show of hands. "Those that had less than twenty correct." The hand attached to the girl who sat on my right did not go up. It should have. Someone's hand went up and there was a brief discussion of how the person on the left should be ashamed of their efforts and ability.

"Those with more than twenty-one but less than forty correct."

My neighbour's hand went up. Miss Stand-In English said this group had to try harder, concentrate more, listen to sounds. I wanted to fucking kill her but stopped myself; I was safe so far.

A show of hands arose for "Greater than forty." The person who had marked my right-hand-side neighbour's work went up. My neighbour knew how to spell and therefore would know how to mark. It dawned on me the person to my right had learned how to cheat for me.

Then, the tables turned. Miss Stand-In English wanted words to show off how good a speller she was. I sat in silence, gathering my breath, my stomach, and my bowels, thankful for getting away with the last task and relieved that it was over.

The activity went on and we asked her to spell words, which she did spell perfectly. The person who suggested the word had to look it up in the Oxford Dictionary to confirm her correct spelling. I remained silent, but my rabbit Thumper crossed my mind. Every year, he went to get his anti-Watership-Down "mixi" injection, as it was known to me. I whispered to my right, "Mixi, the disease rabbits get." She was the vet's daughter as well as being super clever, so I knew she would know what I was talking about.

She did, and she told me the full name was myxomatosis. She confirmed this was hard to spell and said I should ask Miss Stand-In English to spell it. I didn't want to – I didn't want to have to try and find it in the Oxford Dictionary – but said to her, "You can, if you want."

Her hand went into the air. When chosen, she said "myxomatosis."

The owner of the hand then found it in the dictionary and corrected Miss Stand-In English's spelling. It was the first word Miss Stand-In English had spelt incorrectly.

"Well done," she whispered to me.

The bell sounded, next class. I gathered my stuff and headed out the door. Don't fucking mess with me, Miss Stand-In English – I appear to have an abettor.

The following week Miss English was back and the class was discussing death, suicide, bravery, and cowardice. The more I listened to and looked at Hemingway's words, the more I realised that, like myself, he had keen interest in this particular bundle of topics.

Hemingway's *American Henry* recalled a quote, "a coward dies a thousand deaths, the brave but once." His contra-part Catherine claims the brave "dies perhaps two thousand deaths if he's intelligent. He simply doesn't mention them."

Henry's line is a misquote from Shakespeare's *Julius Caesar*: "A coward dies a thousand times before his death, but the valiant taste of death but once." Soon after Caesar makes this statement, he is murdered. It was the early signs that Henry and Catherine were not heading towards a happy-ever-after ending either.

Death in the Afternoon is a confused philosophy of death.

Chapter 39

Many of Hemingway's characters challenge death by fighting in wars, bull-running in Spain, fishing off the Florida coast, or hunting in Africa. But these are Hemingway characters, although based on Hemingway's reality.

Ernest Hemingway had been accident-prone throughout his life. Who survives a plane crash? He survived two in just forty-eight hours. When depressed, paranoid, brain-injured, and bipolar, he was told he had to stop drinking. He was hospitalized and received electroconvulsive shock treatment, and he obeyed and obliged long enough to be discharged. The following morning he donned his emperor's robe, took his favourite double-barrelled shotgun, placed it to his head, and pulled the trigger. Hemingway was successful, renowned, awarded, and decorated due to his writings. He was larger than life, fearless, an American hero living the American dream. But, when he was unable to write, unable to do anything of what he enjoyed in life, of what made life worthy for him, he refused to drink through a non-spill beaker and straw. He refused to wait for death to find him. He pulled the trigger and ended it.

Ernest Hemingway found death. Ernest Hemingway was no coward.

40

Miss English still saw panic hijacking my body at the mention of tests or exams, even though I no longer felt ultimate dread and certain failure when they were brought up. A reader and scribe was Miss English's next negotiation tool to my subconscious hijacker. Someone could read the questions to me, and that same person could write my answers. But was that not cheating? Surely that was what English was, being able to read and write.

Being able to read and write was English, and she said I could do both, but comprehension was more critical. My comprehension was greater when something was spoken, and my spoken vocabulary would always be greater than my written words. Consciously or subconsciously, I did not want spelling errors in my written work. I would write words, but I would speak vocabulary. I could trial doing exams with a reader and scribe; I would even be permitted extra time in the exam in order to complete them. Surely the exam time should be shortened, not lengthened, as someone else was now going to do the time-consuming task of reading and the tiring, endless task of spelling?

Miss English even knew a person who she thought would

Chapter 40

be happy to do this role: Judy Mitchell, someone I'd known for years. She sang in the ceilidh that I danced at every Thursday evening, and she had been kind to me for all that time. She told me I danced beautifully. She had always been very polite and soft-spoken – I'd never noticed her perfectly-spoken English before, only her perfectly-tuned singing. Maybe she could be trusted to keep my shameful secret. What a happy coincidence that Miss English was suggesting someone to read and write for me that I already liked.

"Don't think, sail the course and take what comes."

Yes, I would do a trial exam with Mrs Mitchell reading and scribing.

I thought the trial was a complete disaster, and I said so while talking to Miss English afterwards. It was too easy. The room had Mrs Mitchell, me, and someone hidden in the corner who openly said he was there to ensure there was no cheating and time was kept. The room was quiet – there were no peers coughing, sniffing, huffing, or puffing. I had to ask Mrs Mitchell to read this section or that section. I had to direct her, or she wouldn't do anything. She made notes if I asked, she re-read bits if I asked. She was a little bit like a puppet. When she was writing my thoughts, I had to tell her to do full stops, capital letters, new paragraph. I tested her: if I kept talking, she kept writing on and on and on without any full stops.

My thoughts became uncluttered, not confused with how I was going to adapt my answer to enable me to get something written down. Mrs Mitchell never stalled, never hesitated; I tried harder and harder words, and she could spell them all. None of my answers contained myxomatosis, but I knew she would be able to spell it. Soon, my thoughts were almost solely comprised of my answer; Mrs Mitchell wrote down my vocabulary as it spilled out from between my teeth. It was easy, and if I thought something was easy, then I knew I'd done it wrong. A complete disaster.

Miss English said that I had done extremely well, and that my result was better than most. She considered it so much of a success, she thought I should use Mrs Mitchell as a reader and scribe in all my subjects.

Surely having a reader and scribe was cheating, although somehow it was acceptable cheating. I didn't understand, but I knew tests were easier with Mrs Mitchell. My grades would be better, and I could escape this town sooner with better grades.

"Don't think, sail the course and take what comes."

I would do all my exams with Mrs Mitchell, my reader and scribe.

For my fifteenth birthday, I went to spend the weekend with Evan in Warwick, where he was living in the University Halls of Residence. It was my first solo trip. My parents put me on the train in Aviemore, I changed trains in Edinburgh Waverley station, and then Evan met me at Warwick. The university was bigger than our hometown. Evan had new friends; some were Welsh, some were English. They studied Law, Physics, and Law and Physics. Evan was reading *Pure Maths*. They were all really, really clever, but they were kind to me. They included me in their jokes, in their card games, in their drinking games. They were completely different to the clever people in my class. They never knew of my broken brain – they likely thought I was clever because I was Evan's little sister and looked like him too. People thought we were twins, so my actual age caused no obstacles.

We went to the pub. We spent a lot of time in the uni bar. We went to get pizza. We even went to the supermarket. Evan was independent. I loved it all, I wanted it all, but I knew I'd never be reading Pure Maths or Law. I enjoyed my weekend

Chapter 40

and dreamed of my independence, my freedom, all the way back to Aviemore.

If I wanted to go away to university or college, I'd have to do Highers. I wanted to leave school as soon as possible, which would be after I completed the pending standard grades, but people with standard grades did not go away to university or college. I realised I might have to stay longer at school to achieve a true escape. I could only stay and do Highers if I passed some standard grades though, and I feared I might not get this chance.

Back at school, Mrs Mitchell did all my native-language-based exams with me. I still saw her every Thursday night at the ceilidh and she never mentioned school on these Thursdays; she kept my shameful secret.

Miss English thought I should prepare for Highers and choose which subjects I would like to do them in. I secretly feared that my results from my standard grade would make Highers a non-option.

What would be my options? I was lost, again. Like Prentice in *The Crow Road*, I was lost even within my own family of weirdos. Searching for an identity amongst clues that aren't really clues to anything only succeeded in putting you in the wrong direction. The best ending we can hope for is victory, not happiness. Eventually we will all be away on the Crow Road. This book is fiction but once again it struck me as fact, a scrambled jigsaw puzzle of the events and times that are called "life."

I kept myself busy outside of school. I walked Kerry every day after school, come rain or shine, and I had activities most evenings. I had swimming club on Mondays. Tuesday and Wednesday meant dance practice class, Thursday was ceilidh with Mrs Mitchell, and then show dancing was Friday, Saturday, and Sunday. It kept me from having to try to fit into circles of pretend friends. The majority of my friends had all gone to university at the same time as Evan, as in reality they were Evan's friends that had simply tolerated my presence. It was far easier to buy, write, and post myself a Valentines card than to meet/keep a boyfriend. Valentines cards were important to my mother, so I ensured I got one every year.

There were nights that were not filled up with dancing, and on those evenings I did what my peers did. I walked up and down the high street engaging in conversation and underage drinking, pretending to be interested in the opposite sex. Pretending to be normal. Pretending to fit in. I really needed to get out of this town, or this could be my life.

My father was my usual driver and escort to my dancing events. He stubbornly continued to state his admiration for my skill and confidence in these displays. I knew that he probably only drove me because Mum did not like driving in the dark – she never saw well when faced with oncoming lights – and because my father loved to chat to anyone about anything. He was fascinated by where people were from and stole bits of information from them that they willingly provided.

Hogmanay was always the busiest night for dancing in Scotland. The town was full of people looking for a Scottish Hogmanay, the hotels overbooked and every establishment wanting to show their guests a taste of highland dancing. Everyone had a ceilidh, and every ceilidh was bursting at the seams.

The whole evening was carefully timed and planned. The haggis would be piped in and a Burns expert would deliver the "Address to the Haggis." The pipe band would do a section as would the dancers before the crowd were left to drink too much Speyside whiskey and become experts in Scottish ceilidh

Chapter 40

dancing themselves, Stripping the Willows faster and faster until the early hours. The groups passed each other, going in and out of the different ceilidhs like ships in the night. We dancers always preferred our turn to be completed before the haggis was piped in – gravy spots on the wooden dance floor were responsible for many a person, including myself, slipping and falling on occasion.

For the majority of these shows, the display dancing only involved two people: the piper and the dancer. They are the only two in the room who know what is correct and what is wrong. They are a team who cover each other. On occasion, I would forget or lose the sequence of steps, but all you've got to do is keep hopping in time with the piper's foot, who will now be stamping the beat rather than tapping it until you get back on track, until you remember where you are. The only person who knows for sure you're cheating is the piper, and you can give him a smile and a nod of "it's okay, I'm back on track" on a turn, and he'll slip in a few extra bars to the music so you both finish at the same time. I was an expert cheater with my pipe major. He gave me my nickname of Highland Chancer, but the name did not upset me; he was always just as guilty of cheating as I was.

The Rangers Football Club won their fifth title in a row and were now deemed the most successful Glasgow Rangers team. The players started releasing their autobiographies, and Ally McCosit and Mark Hateley were likely the most feared strikers in the country. The English would argue, as they always did, but the fact hit them hard in early November '92, when the two goals that went past the Leeds keeper and sent them tumbling out of the European Cup were two of the best goals ever witnessed. You could "Ooh Ah Cantona" all you wanted, but it was balls in nets that mattered. Maybe John Lukic could get a few tips from Andy Goram if he ever released his story.

Miss English did not have these books on audiotape; if I wanted to read them, I'd have to actually read them. I preferred reading a book if I knew what was coming, knew what to expect. If I had an idea what direction the story or information was going to take, it permitted my brain to concentrate on the words as it already knew at least part of the story locked within. I read Mark Hateley's autobiography first, since I'd stalked his career so much that I could have partly written it myself. I stood outside the glorious Legoland called Ibrox one Saturday morning where Hateley duly signed it. I then read Ally McCosit's book and collected his signature. I did the same to Richard Gough. I also read the autobiography of Graeme Souness, who had deserted for greener pastures of Liverpool; I never got the chance to collect his signature.

Another year ended, and the swimming gala once again saw me an easy winner. My parents sat at the start/finish line, cheering enthusiastically.

They also sat in the audience as I collected my prize in art and design. I don't know if they clapped and cheered; I never looked. Their past behaviour assured me they would indeed be clapping for all the prize winners, apart from me.

41

I was once again wrong; Highers *were* an open option to me. The brown envelope that dropped through the letterbox showed a list of ones and twos and a three against German, the only subject that I did not do with Mrs Mitchell. According to the breakdown of each subject my top abilities were talking and reading in English (an obvious error, throwing into question whether any of the numbers on this paper could be trusted), investigating in maths, expressive and critical activities in art and design, knowledge and understanding and evaluating in geography, practical abilities in biology, and practical and organisational skills in home economics.

I was fairly certain I had cheated by using my reader and scribe, but it didn't matter. There was some hope in being able to do the Highers. If I could pass some, then I could escape this town.

I called Mrs Mitchell to tell her of our results, and to thank her. She said that she was delighted, but that it was all my work. She asked what Highers I was thinking of doing. I hadn't originally thought of it as a possibility, but I decided I might try English Higher. She said she would be delighted to be my reader and scribe if I wanted her.

I talked to Miss English and she thought pursuing the English Higher was a great idea. She thought I was able to do the Higher with one year of study, although there was the option to study for Highers over two years. She would be teaching the one year Higher and I didn't want to do the two-year option, so one year it was. My next Higher chosen was home economics, which was also deemed a good idea. Four Highers was the maximum you could do, so I chose geography as my third.

I had recently thought of architecture as a career, only because I really liked Charles Rennie MackIntosh and had recently come across Frank Lloyd Wright, who was responsible for adding more United States cities to my must-visit list as well as cementing Hemingway's Oak Park and New York as absolute musts. I had been impressed with Ronda ever since the trip with my family and had since learned that both the New Bridge – or correctly called the Puente Nuevo – and the Plaza de Toros were the creation of the same architect, Jose Martin de Aldehuela. But I couldn't be an architect because I never carried technical drawing through as a standard grade subject, so now I also deserted art and design.

In Highers, the class number more than halved. The majority of my year had chosen to leave the school but not the community. They all worked within the local area and dated local girls whom they would likely marry and have local children with in order to repeat the never-ending cycle of Grantown-on-Spey. Not me – I stayed at school. I worked hard for my Highers. Many of the people who had earned a place on my Not To Be Trusted list, the people I avoided, had taken the option to leave after standard grades.

Shakespeare's *Romeo and Juliet* was the first work of my English Higher. I watched the film a few times then tackled

Chapter 41

the book, stopping and turning to the glossary at every word I didn't know the meaning of. I still preferred the audiobooks, but I was aware I could not have a reader and scribe for the rest of my life; I needed to learn to read for myself. It was slow but thorough work. Shakespeare did write in a different English, but he was consistent in that language. Certain parts of this play were more likely to arise in the exam, and these were discussed at length in class.

This year, I decided to pursue the Gold Duke of Edinburgh award. There were only four of us who wanted to achieve this, two from the current Secondary Six and one other from my Secondary Five. We planned our training expedition and set off to walk fifty miles over five days while carrying everything we would need along the way. I carried a bottle of vodka the whole way without drinking any, too tired to do so following the day trek, setting up camp, and making food.

I was very much in agreement with Prince Charles' understanding of love, as he famously put it – "whatever 'in love' means" – as he was engaged to Lady Spencer. I would never confess to being in love with the boy within our walking group, but I did like him. He was not around for the Primary Three that left me behind; he had moved into the area sometime after that. He may not know how daft I was, but I never risked being rejected, or being made fun of, or being gossiped about by admitting I liked him.

I could explain the opposites of character traits of *Romeo and Juliet*: the passionate, admired, clever Romeo and the rather innocent thirteen-year-old child Juliet. I could explain how they developed – how the hateful/hurtful no-mercy love that accepts no boundaries grew between them, which never had a chance of a happy ending.

We passed our training expedition, meaning that we had not

died and did not require to be rescued, and so we graduated to the actual expedition. We took the Edinburgh train for an hour before getting off at Blair Atholl. It took us five days to walk back through Glen Tilt, Lairig Ghru, Glen Spey, and into Rothiemurchus.

There was a group already set up at our second night campsite when we arrived. The lads wanted to keep walking to the next site which was about one and a half miles away, but the girls wanted to stop for the day. We had to wait for our assessor to ask if we could go on. He appeared about thirty minutes later and said we could go on if we wanted to; the girls didn't, but the boys did. The lads said they would carry our bags so that we only had to walk. It seemed to be a fair trade, so we set off for the next campsite. The double-rucksack lads still led and the girls took up the rear, with the assessor trailing behind us. We got to the next campsite as darkness was falling. The lads collapsed. The girls made food first, which meant the tents would have to go up in the dark. Thankfully, our assessor arrived as we were eating and said we could stay in the bothy. We happily slid into our sleeping bags and chatted in the dark. The vodka was barely touched. I more than liked this boy.

I knew the unusual twofold climax within the usual five act play structure – the exposition, the rising action, the turning point, the falling action and the resolution. The passion and strength to love or hate, of violence and in death, a tragedy but a triumph of human spirit. I knew this play.

Years ago, I was told that repeating Primary Three would benefit me. Eventually, it did. Since I had sprung from the second youngest to one of the oldest kids in my year, I was one of the first to hit the age where I could learn to drive. I was keen to learn, hopeful that a driver's licence would give me some independence. My father was to teach me the basics, as

Chapter 41

he had done with both my brothers. He had a 50/50 success rate, and I was to be the decider.

Calum had eased through the process of learning to drive and securing a licence. He also collected a small tally of off-road trips through fences and into fields, once ending upside down. Evan did not get to the driving test stage – in fact, I think it would be fair to say he did not really get to the driving stage. He did get to the obsessive mirror-checking stage, to the point he overlooked the big window in the front and crashed into a pile of road salt, although it is important to note that I was not there and stories are usually adapted over time. Evan had not been as eager to learn to drive as his friends, who had rushed out and gained their licence and were more than happy to collect and drop Evan off as he required.

Evan was chauffeured; no one would chauffeur me. I knew that if I wanted to go anywhere, I was going to have to drive myself.

I found learning to drive quite boring. It seemed an eternity before Father permitted me onto the actual road. My first, second, and third lessons were to dip the clutch into first, press on the accelerator and find biting point, move slowly forward and stop as we had reached the end of the drive. Then dip clutch and into reverse, find the biting point, slowly move backwards and stop. This went on and on and on and on. What the hell did this have to do with getting anywhere? This back and forth up and down the drive was pointless as far as I was concerned, and it reminded me of so many other aspects of my life, such as the reading homework that was done but appeared not done the next day, only to be repeated and repeated day after day as if a different result would magically appear. But back and forth I went, up and down the drive as instructed by father, listening for and then holding the infamous biting point, hoping that nobody would pass and recognise me. I tried not to imagine what would be said if it was found out that I was so poor at driving that my own family would not allow me to drive on the road.

My parents constantly reminded me of the dangers of speed and the open road, of the deaths of people I knew, families hurt and parents who never recovered from their child's passing. Both my brothers had lost friends in fatal car accidents. The roads were dangerous, I understood that, but I couldn't stay on the driveway forever.

I finally graduated onto the road, and then graduated to my test and passed first try. I was ready for every car to pull out/turn/stop in front of me. I was prepared for the unexpected, for the thing you think is least likely to happen. This was how I prepared for life, not just for driving.

I once swerved in an attempt to avoid hitting a deer, although I did end up hitting it lightly. Father, who was my passenger, was angry at me for crossing the white line. He lifted the deer over the fence and received a full kick to his arm. As we watched it bound away, I received the Dangers of Driving lecture again, which now included mowing down animals. I said I wouldn't kill animals, and therefore I'd not drive. He made me drive home anyways, and we never mentioned the deer again. I kept an eye on his arm through its different stages of purples and yellows over the next ten days, comforted that the deer had bounded away apparently uninjured.

A boy who had never been cruel to me, who was always assured a certain seat at the clever table, who was also the second male in my Duke of Edinburgh team, failed his driving test. Silly me – I voiced my approval that he had failed and received a stern lecture from Mother about wishing ill on people and how I had been brought up better than that. I did not bother to explain

Chapter 41

that I did not wish him ill or even dead – he was not on my list – but I was pleased that for once everything was not super easy for him, that he could experience the bitter taste of failure.

I now had the freedom of a driving licence and willingly became one of Evan's chauffeurs. Oftentimes I visited the Alvie churchyard, sometimes with flowers but mostly not. I had never really known my Auntie Nina, never spent any time with her alone. I sat in that churchyard looking at those two identical stones, knowing that animals had benefited from her donations, recalling the never-ending curly kale for Thumper. Now aware of the effort and care she provided to her parents while trying to keep her family together when she was just a child herself, I thought I rather liked this oddball of an aunt. She stood up for what she believed and wanted. She fought hard. She chose what she shared and what she kept to herself. She had won; she was resting and decomposing exactly where she wanted to be. I had nothing but admiration for this lady.

Nobody could argue that this pair had not chosen a magnificent spot. If I ever required the use of a church, it would be this one: Alvie Church within the Alvie churchyard.

42

In my English Higher, we studied William Wordsworth's *Prelude* and William Shakespeare's *Sonnets*. We would have to learn one of these collections of works, and I was a fan of the latter. Plus, I was already familiar with Shakespearean English.

For my birthday, I again went to visit Evan at Warwick where he was now in his second year, flatting and living in Leamington Spa. His group of friends were mostly the same as the previous year; he was good at keeping friends.

Evan took me to Stratford upon Avon for a day, the home of William Shakespeare, where we visited his birthplace. Here I found a book of the sonnets that had the sonnet on one page and a translation into today's language on the facing page, as well as comments, notes, and thinking points on a few pages that followed. I flicked straight to sonnet 116, where the pages revealed everything I had a learned at school and more. When Evan was finished looking at whatever he was investigating I put the book down, and then Evan picked it up and added it to his pile for purchase.

We visited the Windmill, the Church of the Holy Trinity, and Shakespeare's resting place before spending the remainder of the day at the Dirty Duck alehouse.

Chapter 42

I worked my way slowly – or thoroughly, as I like to think of my reading and understanding speed – through the sonnets, from "we desire that all created things may grow more plentiful" to "Love's fire heats water, but water doesn't cool love."

We want to believe that sonnet 116 is true. We want to believe that love conquers all, and by Shakespeare's own words, if this be proven as an error, then none of his writings are true. But if this is not an error, then are the other sonnets true? Are these a biography, like the "Prelude" is to Wordsworth?

Did Shakespeare love a man? Or, was he just obsessed over a man? Who is the dark lady, who he knows is not true to him but who accepts his aging? Why does his wife Anne not appear in any sonnets? Was his wife real life and his writing his dream life, his imagination, his escape to a better place? I didn't know. Miss English did not either when I asked her. Nobody knows.

I continued to fill my time with highland dancing, and now I was making money. There was prize money from the competitions, but far more lucrative was the show dancing. Hogmanay was the best earner of the year, followed closely by the unofficial Scottish national day, January 25, Rabbie's birthday. I did not care for "To a Mouse," never spent much time on the "Address to a Haggis," but the world sang "Auld Lang Syne" to welcome the New Year, even if they didn't know who wrote it or the correct moment within the tune to cross your arms.

The other girls would spend their money on clothes, makeup, and music, but I had no need for any of that. My mother bought my clothes. I did not wear makeup – it was tested on innocent bunny rabbits. And as for music, whatever my brothers listened to was fine, or there was always Mum and Dad's choice of country or western. "Here I go again, once again, with a suitcase in my hand…" How those words never left me. I said I liked the song, but it was the image I liked. Here I go again, with a suitcase in my hand – would it ever be my turn? I popped my dancing money in the bank, then popped the next lot in and the next lot. I had three thousand pounds. I could have bought a car, but I already used Mum's car. I saved, although I did not know what for.

Exam time came once again, and once again I hid in the little room by the library with Mrs Mitchell and the silent observer. I flicked through the first section of pages of Higher English. I was looking at the English passages, hoping that I would recognise one. And then, there it was: Act two, scene two.

"*O Romeo, Romeo! wherefore art thou Romeo?*
Deny thy father and refuse thy name;
Or, if thou wilt not, be but sworn my love,
And I'll no longer be a Capulet."

I knew this scene. It didn't matter what the question was, I would be answering it.

I needed to answer a question in section two as well, so I kept turning the pages and asked Mrs Mitchell to read bits of the different questions. When she finished reading one I asked her to stop and said I wanted her to write something. When she got her pen I took a big breath and started dictating.

"Let me not to the marriage of true minds new line admit impediments full stop, love is not love new line which alters when it alteration finds full stop, new line or bends with the remover to remove colon new line or no semicolon, it is an ever-fixed mark comma new line that looks on tempests comma and is never shaken semicolon new line, it is the star to every wandering bark comma new line whose worth's unknown comma although his height be taken full stop new line, love's not time's fool comma though rosy lips and cheeks new line within his bending sickle's compass come semicolon new line,

Chapter 42

love alters not with his brief hours and weeks comma new line, but bears it out even to the edge of doom full stop new line, if this be error and upon me proved comma new line I never writ comma nor no man ever loved full stop."

I'd need this to answer the question she had just read out. I had forgotten the capital letters, but this was only notes so I could add them later if needed. I stopped and turned back to the start of the paper, wondering if it was wise to answer my two questions on the same author.

I asked Mrs Mitchell to read all the questions as I pondered this dilemma. I could answer these two Shakespeare questions, but if I wasn't going to use Shakespeare for both, which one would I drop and what I would replace it with? I had neither answer by the time Mrs Mitchell had finished reading the questions. There were possibilities, but Shakespeare was my strongest. I decided to answer my two questions about the same author.

The end of the school year approached and the Glasgow Rangers won their sixth title in a row. The effort was huge, though crushing injuries riddled the team – by the end, there were more players requiring surgery than players not. I collected my now-usual swimming trophy, even though I was now in the senior year and had to swim against the year that was above me.

During the prize-giving ceremony, I walked on stage when my name was called and collected my prize in English. Miss English was clapping madly. My parents were present as always and said how proud they were of me, delivering another line from the parenting must-use lines to support a child, a text I knew almost as well as they did.

When I walked back down the steps and off the stage, I wanted to continue walking out of the school and all the way to my primary school. I wanted to parade the English prize around like the others were allowed to parade their dancing trophies. I wanted to slam it down on Miss Primary Six's desk. I wanted to tell her exactly how fucking dreadful her teaching was. That this prize was nothing to do her efforts. That she should be ashamed of herself. Her input in my education was not teaching, it was belittling and bullying. I could say I was dumbfounded by how she was able to sleep at night. I wanted to shout and scream at her, like she had done to me so often. I wanted to tell her how pathetic she was, beating up on kids to make herself feel better. She was mental – she needed psychiatric help. But my mum said I could not go and show my prize off, and I had only given her the acceptable side of what I would do on my English prize school tour.

I didn't conduct the tour, not because Mum said no but because it's always best not to count one's chickens before they hatch. I might have a prize from a teacher who spent a lot of time with me, but my Shakespeare results were still to be marked and reported. I still might have failed English. I likely *had* failed, as I answered Shakespeare to both questions. So instead, I settled on rehearsing the scene over and over and over again in my mind. I would make her cry like a baby. She had won many battles due to her seniority, but she needed to be told that I had won the fucking war.

43

The brown envelope containing my Higher results fell through the slot in the front door, and I took it to my room. Mum and Dad were out working. Evan was home for summer semester break, but he was asleep. It was just me, my tears, my sweat, my future, my effort, and the fear that what lay in the envelope would decide if I was ever going to escape. I was shaking, crying, trying to breathe. The piece of paper came out face down and I couldn't turn it over, riddled by the fear of failure.

I stared at the paper, willing to be able to see through it. I closed my eyes and turned the paper over. I sat there for a long time, dreaming. I even tried praying for the first time in years.

On the right hand side of the paper, in a neat column, were the grades. There were no Ds for Dunderhead. Instead there were passes, all passes. I scanned the column again and again – definitely no dunderhead Ds. There were As and Bs where there should have been Ds.

I was dizzy, I needed some water. I walked down the long corridor of our house numb, dazed, dumbfounded even. Then, as I was the furthermost point from the piece of paper it dawned on me. I had received the wrong results. It was someone else's results. They had mixed up. Someone else would be crying over a column of Ds until they realised they were looking at the wrong results.

I went back and checked the name at the top of the paper, which seemed to confirm that these marks indeed belonged to Rhona Esther Macdonald.

It was finished. I was safe. I had passed. I was leaving. I could escape.

I went to Evan's room to say I was leaving; I'd passed. He looked at the paper with me. He confirmed I was out of here and added that in fact I'd achieved a better grade in English than he had.

I called my reader and scribe to share my unbelievable news. She sounded pleased, almost proud of our work, or my work as she kept correcting me. The truth is I doubt I could have done it without her, without our little room by the library and the mute observer who sat behind us.

I had no new career ideas, other than being an architect which was clearly not a possibility. However, my Auntie in Australia was a nurse and she had worked in London, Colombo in Ceylon and Sydney. I realised I might be able to collect passport stamps as a nurse, and this was very attractive to me.

When I was very small, my eldest brother was cycling home from swimming when his bag went into his front wheel spokes and he went over the handlebars, cutting his chin wide open. Mum took him to the hospital – with Evan and me in tow, as Father was working – where they laid Calum down under a bright light and took out a needle and thread. I apparently wriggled off Mum's knee and got myself to a better vantage point, where I silently, motionlessly, watching them sew Calum's chin back together. They had said at the time I should be a nurse, and I now decided that is exactly what I would do: become a nurse and see the world.

Chapter 43

Father seemed to approve, although if you think about it nursing is not unlike air hostessing. Nurses give out food and collect trays. They use oxygen and deal with life and death emergencies. The main difference I could think of was air hostess got to travel the world while nurses got to clean up poo.

I didn't hugely care where I went for schooling so long as it was away from here. My year group were mostly aiming for the Edinburgh unitechs and university, or the ones not so eager to pack up and leave headed the shorter distance of Aberdeen. I neither wanted to be close to our sleepy town nor close to my peers, so I set my heart on Glasgow.

Glasgow was a great city, a city of new growth. The tenements with public wash houses were getting demolished; they had been unfit to live in when my father was there in the '40s but it took until the '90s to pull them down. It was home to Glasgow Rangers Football Club and Charles Rennie MackIntosh.

I applied for training at the Royal Infirmary. It was an impressive building with an impressive history, claiming to have employed workers who set up the first radiology department and pioneered the use of ultrasound. My training would be fifty percent on the wards and fifty percent in the classroom. This gave me hope – my classroom work would only be one-and-a-half of the next three years. Maybe I could get through that. However, I had to get a place first. I had to interview and persuade them why they should give me a place and not someone else.

Interview preparation followed the same routine of pre-exam preparations. As I sat on the train to Glasgow I felt relieved and content, temporarily satisfied with my travel. But, as I walked into the interview I felt sick, my stomach shouting as if it belonged to a child in Ethiopia, my bowels rolling and shaking like the San Andreas plate. I felt like a fraud. I wasn't clever. No one would ever let me be a nurse and give me the responsibility of another person's life.

The interview was hazy and confusing, not unlike the feeling of looking at unknown words in your own handwriting as you stand at the teacher's desk, but I would not have to come back and repeat this tomorrow or the next day. If I could get this correct the first time, I could have a place in nursing college.

I tried to stay positive. I told myself I had done well, that I'd given good answers to their questions. On returning home, I said it had gone well and commenced the long wait for the letter, which would either support my story or make me a liar.

My Duke who had carried two rucksacks was leaving – he was off to Edinburgh. He barely knew who I was, other than the girl who once took a compass bearing on a sheep when she thought it was a white rock. His whole year was leaving, off to university. If I'd not repeated Primary Three, I could have been in that group. But I did repeat Primary Three, so I was not leaving, I was staying. At least for now.

44

The letter came. I was a liar. It said no, that I was not mature enough. Déjà vu, Primary Three.

Mum found a pre-nursing course in Perth and helped me apply. Mother had a fondness for Perth and its surrounding area, the fair city, the gateway to the Highlands. I was never convinced of its charm; the place just seemed small and quiet. I wanted to get further than just the gateway, but it could be a step in the right direction.

This interview went surprisingly well; I didn't even have to lie to myself about how well it went. The pre-nursing course was a year, then I would get into the Glasgow Royal Infirmary. I just needed the letter to confirm my plan was set.

The letter came and my exit plan was once again shredded. It said no, that I would not benefit from the course. It said I was too clever. Inconceivable!!

I had failed. I was a failure, again. I had failed to escape. Not clever enough, but also too clever. It was draining. I couldn't understand what had happened. I had to go back to school.

I knew my Do Not Eat canister was useless; it may have worked when I was smaller, or more likely would have made me ill and caused a never-ending list of questions from the adults. But I still had it – it still lived in its hidden place within my bedroom.

Everyone is lonely in *A Clean, Well-Lighted Place* – the old man drinking, the older waiter, the uniform man and his evening's entertainment. They are all sad in their differing ways, all lonely apart from one overconfident young waiter who believes he has it all – a wife, a job, youth – and that his hour is more important than the old, lonely, suicidal man who drinks brandy in the well-lit place rather than at a bar or alone. Everyone is lonely in an "all men are equal, but some are more equal than others" kind of way.

Why did Hemingway make these lonely people so fearful of bed, so frightened of their thoughts, of being by oneself? Hemingway's old man in the sea was such the opposite – that old man claimed "And bed, he thought. Bed is my friend. Just bed, he thought. Bed will be a great thing." That man longed for bed, just as I did.

45

Unable to leave, I was now in the most senior year at secondary school. We were also the weakest year; at only seven pupils, we were vastly outnumbered by the other year groups. I had no enemies within the seven, but that's not to say we were the Secret Seven. There were still a few I was cautious of, my armour and guard remaining firmly in place.

I did two Highers: biology, and my formerly abandoned subject of art and design. I loved one and remained terrified of the other one's teacher, complete with his wonky eye.

One of the seven was a friend. She had sat beside me for most of the worst years of my life – my goddess who had no confidence in the water, the girl who read books by torchlight under the blankets when I just hid in my bed. She was undoubtedly one of the cleverest people in the class. She was also kind, considerate, and polite. She even shared her friend with me so I actually might have two friends. She wanted to be a doctor. I sat beside her in biology. In art and design, I sat beside her friend who by default was also my friend.

My non-swimmer, reader-under-the-sheets friend had done more than never tease me, she had tried to help me. It was never her fault that she gave me a word that I could not read;

she must have thought I was able to read more than I could. I never blamed her, I blamed myself for the screaming that resulted in not only my tears but also hers. More successfully, she helped me through Miss Stand-in English's classes. I don't think we knew we were friends then, we never ever attended each other's birthday parties, but maybe we were friends now.

I quickly learned that these subjects were not going to help me. Art and design was useless to me without technical drawing. Becoming an architect was as much of a dream as conservation work in Africa. I would never pass biology as the teacher was unreadable and unpredictable – I spent most of my time in class trying to be ready for his next outburst, and so I did not spend much time on the biology books. I was tired. Where was my Crow Road?

I struggled on; there was no other option. Like the old people in the formal grand hotel, I had to wait my time, wait to be chosen. Wait for my never-ending sleep.

One day, I was invited to a party. The usual accepted term would be that friends had invited me to their party, into their cult, into something I'd never been a part of. I felt warmed, encouraged, honoured, and flattered that this was going to be my reckoning. I wasn't going to complete my escape, so I better get to know these people. This was to be the beginning of the new me – the popular, liked, wanted me. This was a fresh start.

I spent considerable amounts of time getting ready, just as Calum had demonstrated many times, forbidding access to the bathroom to everyone else in the house. I was actually rather bored with the idea of going out by the time I was able to complete my grooming. I even wore makeup – some rabbit would have had this goop stuffed into its eyes to see if it reacted. But the fact remained that I had been invited, and I had accepted, and therefore I had to condition myself to the

Chapter 45

rules. I accepted the animal abuse. I wondered if they made makeup that was not tested on rabbits and made a mental note to look into this further.

I tried on every scrap of clothing I owned, some twice, the discarded pile of clothes growing greater than a week's washing, before retrying the discarded pile and then discarding them again.

My brother warned me about arriving at a party too early, and how such a basic error could lead me into awkward conversations with people you would not normally talk with. Although I would not normally have spoken to any of the people I was expecting to see at this party, this was part of the reason I wanted to attend – it could be a new group of friends just waiting to invite me into their circle. I was prepared for awkward conversations; I was so familiar with awkward conversations that any other type of conversation would be awkward. Awkward was all I knew, so it was a safe fail/fail situation. But I went prepared, so I thought, for the awkwardness.

It turned out I knew several people and was able to talk with them without too much discomfort, and what discomfort I did feel was able to be doused with alcohol. The talk changed from alcohol to drugs and older kids and the imminent arrival of both. This was way out from my comfort zone, but it was too early to go home. My parents would want details of the party – who, what, and why.

I opted to take a bathroom break. My mind was swirling, bad memories overflowing each other; every time my mind turned, it ran into an even worse memory. I couldn't think of a single positive, there was no glimmer of hope. Life would just push and push me until I broke, unable to go on, unwilling to go on. Was this the night?

I should have realised that a bathroom is not the ideal place to hide at a party. People were knocking on the door demanding in, demanding my safe place. I collected a razor and vacated, acquired a drink, and stood against a wall assessing what life had dealt me. I was in a roomful of people who were now willing to invite me to parties and to talk to me, but they had also made my earlier years miserable. This was what I thought I had wanted for a long time, but was this their apology? Inviting me into their clique? It was rubbish. As I looked around and saw their faces, I could feel every ping of pain they had caused. They disgusted me, and I disgusted myself for standing there at their party as if to say, "Hey, it's cool, I understand that you were a bit bored and far cleverer than I'll ever be. You just thought you would kick me around a few years from group to group until I was deflated, punched, and broken."

I found a bedroom and sat on the bed, listening to the noise as it grew like a comedy show that gets funnier and funnier, where you laugh because the person beside you laughs and not necessarily because what was said was humorous. Since the snowball/not snowballs incident, my own family, who I had once trusted, now thought I was a liar, jealous, an unrealistic and silly girl. They belonged in the party having fun, conspiring on their next move to make me feel worse.

What is the worst one person can feel, time and time again? I had been convinced that this was the worst I'd ever feel, and time after time life proved that yet again I was wrong and I could, in fact, feel worse. I had yearned to escape all my life, but I never seemed to get closer; every time I felt like I was almost there, something changed. Too clever for pre-nursing, what the fuck is that about? I was daft, I'd been stupid and gullible all my miserable fucking life.

So what if I won a prize in English? Miss English had pitied

Chapter 45

me for years. The prize was useless to me, I couldn't even slap my Primary Six teacher in the face with it. It didn't get me out of this shitty town.

There is no God. Or, worse still, what if there is a God? He's not looking after me, he's never done a fucking thing to help me, he's done the opposite. The footstep poem about him carrying me when there's only one set of footprints – utter rubbish. Bad things happen because Adam ate the apple – bollocks, utter fucking bollocks. I'm never going to be free; I'll never make it out alive. It's time to break on through to the other side, and if I meet the maker I have a list of fucking questions.

I pushed the razor into my left wrist and discovered that skin is a lot tougher than I had given it credit for. When I fell and grazed my knees or elbows it tore off easily, and paper cuts it when drawn across. But when something sharp is pushed against it, it just bends and contains the red stuff I sought. Maybe that wrist was faulty; after all, I'm faulty.

I switched arms and tried the other wrist. I sawed back and forth a little at that wrist and saw a little red stuff, but it was fairly clear this was going to be harder than I had anticipated. I tried to formulate a new plan. If I was going to do this I'd need to cut both wrists, but that was going to take a lot of sawing and I only had a poxy razor.

This was suicide, what I was doing. I should have done this years ago, before I had fought through so many years. Was it the brave or the cowardly who did this? I had deemed Ernest Hemingway brave, but the longer I sat there the more I knew I was anything but. I was daft. I was a coward. My father said you have to make the best of what you have – is this the best I could do? My dreams told me I could do more, but dreams are unrealistic. That's why they are called dreams. So I sat there, alone with the demons of my thoughts, now aware I'd never escape them. Once again, I was an utter failure. Where to from here?

The door burst open and a crowd of people clamoured in, expecting to find friends in too close a position. I'm too slow to hide the razor and my wrists that actually now both look quite red. I leave and start to walk home – a few followed me, shouting at me, one asking what I thought it was like for them to go to their partners and say they were pregnant at fifteen years old. I don't give a flying fuck about her, or her bastard baby. She, the one who is right this second pretending to care about my wellbeing, was a past ringleader in my torment. She had invited me to a fight, which I never attended but possibly should have. She would have kicked the living daylights out of me, and if she hadn't her rottweiler friends would have finished the job.

I continued to walk home, and eventually they lost interest and left me to it. I arrived home to the expected questions, which I successfully side-stepped, and headed to bed. It dawned on me that Miss Blabbermouth would have told the entire town by now, and that meant that some form of the truth will filter back to my parents – experience had told me that stories that filter through a number of people are never flattering. I got dressed and headed back out. If people saw me they might discount the rumours, or at least not believe them in their entirety.

Only one person confronted me and said, "I heard you were dead." I replied, "Don't believe everything you hear." I could sense that many people were whispering behind my back, but it was difficult to know about what exactly; they were always whispering about something.

I woke up content that my damage control mission had been a success, so I headed to the hill for a snowboarding class. I

Chapter 45

collected my two friends and did not mention the fact that I had betrayed their friendship by attending the party. The day had beautiful clear blue skies and powdery snow. I did so much better with both my feet attached to the same sliding thing than I ever had when they were attached to separate sliding things.

Monday and Tuesday passed uneventfully, and I slowly felt myself slipping back into the coma which was my life.

On Wednesday I was summoned to the dining room. Mother was in tears. It was time to answer for my latest failure.

I had brought great shame to my family; we were the gossip of the town. How could I do this to them? *The town thought, my family did, my town this, my family that,* on and on and on. My mother could not even say "suicide," let alone talk about it. She was disappointed, afraid, and ashamed. I was completely and utterly exhausted.

I tried to explain my side, my miserable, unfair life. Like how I'm not allowed to tell the truth, how I get into trouble because it's not the correct thing to say. It is okay for her to lie and say what one thinks is expected, but I want to be able to tell the truth. I was doomed. I would never win. I hated this town, I hated school, I hated my family, and most of all I despised myself.

She was really crying now – I'd gone too far. Thank god I never told her that I've dreamed of dying/being killed/killing myself for as long as I can remember.

They said I had been given everything I had ever wanted, that I was in fact spoilt. My view was that they never stood up for me, never trusted me, and never believed in me. They just fed me unrealistic lines. "You can do anything with effort." "We're so proud of you." Their lines were lies, but yet lying is supposed to be wrong.

Through all this, we never talked about the actual taboo subject: suicide. Just like Jig's abortion in *Hills Like White Elephants* is not talked about. They talked about drinks, not the actual problem. Likewise, I said the appropriate things about my equivalent of drinks and they took the dominant lead. They talked again and again about the shame I brought on the family name, about my selfishness, about how they had done anything and everything for me. The elephant in the room went ignored, unwanted, misunderstood, unsupported, unloved.

Just when you think life can't get worse, it does. I was done. I had no fight left. I was slurping tea through a no-spill beaker, and I was going to be slurping for years to come. I admitted defeat and surrendered.

There was no point in trying. No point in dreaming of a future. I slept and slept and slept. I had never been so tired.

46

The evening event was never spoken of at school, or at least never spoken to me, likely because very few people from school were at the party. Life slowly returned to its slurping noise. Biology was a struggle, the textbooks heavier in more than just weight. Art and design was fun but pointless.

I completed my community service as part of my Gold Duke of Edinburgh Award Scheme. I volunteered in an old folks home, a former grand house – although not as grand a hotel as the one I'd completed my work experience in. I wanted to see if they were the same. They were very similar but this house was brighter, with fresh air blowing through some windows and a lovely garden we could take the wheelchair residents to sit in and watch life fly around them. Not every meal was cold scrambled eggs, and they got pudding. But they still wore nappies, and their long tongues still met the forks and spoons. They too were waiting for the okay to go down the Crow Road. I did the required amount of time but failed to keep a diary of it, and therefore I never gained my Gold Duke of Edinburgh.

Exams came and passed painfully. I loved my drawing of the broken glass in front of a Jack Daniels bottle with a screwed-up cola can, the pieces reflecting in each other, symbolising bitter pain and disappointment. I really wanted to keep it, but the drawing had to be submitted to the exam board. Biology was my final exam, the last one during my schooling years. I walked home afterwards a little dazed, wondering if I had truly understood those questions or if this was the same feeling that I'd done okay at something only for my results to show that I had completely misunderstood all of the instructions.

I sat on the wall that ran by the path. The sports fields were empty and the school looked deserted; nothing was moving. I sat in the sun and let the peace wash over me. This was exactly the same feeling I had had in Primary Two, when I stupidly thought everyone had been raptured and that I was the only person who remained. I knew it wasn't true today, but I let the feeling wash over me for a while before continuing my final walk home. I wouldn't be coming back here.

My school peers were selecting courses and applying to universities. How could I be successful with the addition of a pass in art and fail in biology? It was too tiring to think about. All I could do was to keep slurping and wait for the Crow Road.

47

The Organisation Queen was in action again. Mum read through the different hospitals, different communities, and different cities I had been looking at the year before. Glasgow was still preferred by me as Edinburgh and Aberdeen were still favoured by the others. The fifty percent in class, fifty percent in placement setting that Glasgow Royal had up for offer the year before was still my first choice. She found a few more options, and I sat numbly in the dining room as she explained them.

My favourite involved a course with two hospitals: Paisley Royal Alexandria and Glasgow Southern General. The community settings included the luxurious Bridge of Weir, where the famous Glasgow Ranger players relaxed in their homes, and the infamous Ferguslie Park, the well-published "shittiest place in Scotland to be dragged up." Or, as the news reports it, "Ferguslie Park is the most deprived area in Scotland."

Father did not want me to have anything to do with Ferguslie Park and therefore, by default, nothing to do with Bridge of Weir, Southern General, or Royal Alexandria. The Auntie who looked after him once he was orphaned was a resident of Possil Park, an area that competed with Ferguslie Park for the status of being the worst. Father preferred my second choice of Ninewells and Dundee.

Mother completed a photocopied application, and I copied it into my own handwriting and sent it off. On Mum's form she had ticked yes to "Ever had a general anaesthetic," and I enquired about the details. I learned that when I was three and a half, I stole one of my brother's chocolates which was wrapped in tinfoil so as to appear to be a football. A few months later, my nostril appeared to have developed a growth. I was taken to the GP and then referred to an ear, nose, and throat specialist whose course of treatment was to anaesthetise me and surgically remove the growth, which turned out to be a small ball of paper with black and white hexagons and pentagons. My parents recognised that this bit of paper once contained the chocolate which I had been told I couldn't have months ago. No one was angry at my theft; instead, they were relieved at the innocence of the growth. It was my first admission and overnight stay in hospital, and I made the connection that my vivid memory of crying while standing at the end of a cot can be attributed to this event.

I continued to copy the application form, but while in bed I thought about the story. My mother was wrong when she claimed that she never left me, that my cries never went unanswered. They left me in hospital. When visiting hours were officially over they left me in a cot, in a row of cots, and no one answered my cries that day. As I thought about it, I realized that this memory is my first memory. My first memory is of being abandoned.

Weeks later, I was back on the train heading to a wet and windy Glasgow, but I didn't care about weather. I stayed in the nurses' home the night before the interview and hid in the tiny, cold room, fearful of having to talk to anyone. I heard

Chapter 47

them going on duty, coming home, getting ready to go out, going out and returning, then getting ready to go back to work. They sounded like they were having fun. They sounded like they were friends.

My new TV show was *ER*, and I thought I could maybe be an emergency room nurse. The patients were all dying or dead anyway – no one would notice if I fucked up and killed someone. I wanted that. I wanted to have fun and have friends. I wanted to be in a nursing home, and not the sort of nursing homes my hometown offered.

I had passed Highers, and I was too clever for pre-nursing. I just needed to believe it, or at least pretend I wasn't stupid; whichever one was easier. I walked in tall, proud, and confident, three things that were far removed from my internal reality.

I was asked to go for a medical examination following my interview. I managed to find the place and wondered if doing so was a test in itself. My blood pressure was taken and the machine popped up with a couple of numbers: seventy and fifty-four. The machine went crazy. The nurse asked if I had eaten breakfast – nope, I was too nervous or scared. She got me some tea and a biscuit and we completed the test. She redid my blood pressure, which now recorded at ninety-nine and sixty. She said that was better and that someone would be in touch.

The Glasgow Rangers collected their seventh title in a row, but the win of the year was overshadowed by Davie Cooper's cerebral haemorrhage and death before his fortieth birthday. I won the senior swimming championship again, but it was not really a win. A junior girl who had popped up a level into the seniors was faster than me and finished first in all four races. I was second in all of them, a mark of failure four times over in one evening. We were the only two swimming in that age group, all others saving themselves from the disgrace. She was deemed to have completed an illegal turn in the first race – I had seen her red ping pong bat and knew before that first race was completed that I could come last in every race and still win the championship. She came and sat beside me after the first race and told me this, thinking it would be news to me. I acted surprised; it was best not to admit to anything.

It was the only gala my parents did not attend; their non-attendance had been at my request. The junior girl had been much faster than me in all the training sessions, and I wanted to save them the humiliation of watching me lose in the one thing I used to be good at. Calum tried to assure me that the ping-pong-bat-holder would not have done me any favours despite him being one of the trainers in the Monday night swim training. He was a seemingly straight up and down honest guy, and he would have given me a red bat if I deserved it. But it never stopped me from wondering, never slowed my mind.

Instead of pursuing the truth, which would have been impossible to find, I just stopped talking about it. I was pleased I'd won, but I would have liked to have seen a video tape of her turn. I'm sure she would have liked to have seen a tape of her turn too.

An envelope addressed to me arrived. My brain knew what it was and hit instant panic. I still had no control over my brain – it controlled me. My thoughts were overrun with "what if" scenarios, the negative ones spiralling out of control. The dog and I opened it together, sat on my bedroom floor. I showed the dog the words, but she was as much help as I'd expected. I turned it around and scanned the words, then rescanned the words as I did not trust my eyes. They sometimes only saw what they wanted to see, but today the words were actually there.

"Pleased."

Chapter 47

"Accepted."

"March 1996."

The words in between were unimportant and unnecessary for my understanding of the content of the letter.

The in-between words explained that they were pleased to be able to advise me of my acceptance to the March '96 nursing intake. It was not conditional to my pending results. It did not matter if I'd passed or failed my recently sat exams. I was in. I had a place in nursing in March of next year.

It was May, and I had a place in nursing school in March. What was I going to do? My peers were already collecting summer jobs to save money for college, but I had already saved £4000 from my dancing. I had money, and I had time.

I would go to Australia.

Mum helped again. We sat in the same dining room where I used to painfully practise my reading and we read the information that had been delivered in the day's post. We also read about flight tickets and tours and bus passes.

During one of these planning evenings, Mum told me about an old neighbour who had said to Mother years ago that no child should be that upset going to school, that it wasn't right. All I could do with this new information was agree and wonder why Mum had not done anything. Maybe she did, maybe she didn't. I never saw any evidence that she did anything other than continue sending me to the torture chambers of primary school. I know my morning routine upset her; I saw tears in her eyes through my own. She would have spoken to Dad about this and a neighbour had spoken to her, but nothing changed.

I had gone to school even though I didn't want to, but now I was going to Australia because I did.

Mum wrote to family in Australia to see if they could give me a meal and bed for the night, and they all wrote back saying they would be delighted to have me. Sydney would be my base as Auntie Helen was there. I had a Greyhound hop-on-hop-off bus pass which took me from Sydney to Canberra, Melbourne, Adelaide, Alice Springs, Darwin, Cairns, Brisbane, and back to Sydney. There were hundreds of other towns I could visit that I knew nothing about as of yet – I would have to read my *Lonely Planet* guidebook to find out which ones I wanted to stop at. I could visit them all, or if I was frightened or hated it I could sit on the bus for days on end and eventually get back to Sydney.

The brown envelope containing my Higher results dropped through the letterbox, not filled with as much fear as previous envelopes. I had a place in nursing college and I was close to having a ticket to Australia. I was leaving this town regardless.

The brown envelope revealed a B and C, no D's. Incredibly, I had passed biology. I'd not failed at anything, other than the subjects that I dropped years ago because they were too hard.

I was told at school that I could do something more than nursing. Animals, I still wanted to work with animals, ideally in Africa, though I was told that meant veterinary studies and that would be difficult with my lack of sciences. It would also be seven years of further classroom and homework. That felt like it might consume the rest my life. If I was too clever for nursing, I didn't care.

I still wanted to work with animals, but I wanted out more. I wanted to be finished. I wanted to be independent, and I wanted to be collecting stamps on my passport. And I was going to make that happen.

48

Once again, I sat on a train within the London Underground on the Piccadilly Heathrow-bound line. It had always been my favourite line; the left-hand end of the line ended in escape, and with it, hope. I even liked the purple colour.

As I sat on the train, my mind drifted back to when I was five and my name was pulled out as the winner of the Christmas pantomime competition, the prize being a trip to London on the Flying Scotsman and accommodation at London's prestigious Grosvenor House Hotel. I didn't recall entering the competition, and I don't really recall much of the trip, but it was my first trip to London. Mum took me and my brothers – it was her first trip to London too. I recall that I had to hold her hand, Evan had to hold her other hand, and Calum had to hold Evan's. We had to be linked at all times, no exceptions, unless we had direct permission to unlink, like when we spent the afternoon in Hamleys, the largest toy shop in the world. The toy shop was mega; London was mega plus. I recall the cabbies being chatty and friendly and the people we shared the pavement with being busy and content in being self-absorbed in their own lives. Nobody talked to each other. I found the loneliness comforting and warming.

My mind made its way back to the present, and I once again looked around at my carriage companions. I'd spent years with my head down looking at their shoes, but today, armed with my airline ticket that would take me far away, I raised my eyes and my head to meet their faces. Not many looked back; just like that first trip to London, everyone was absorbed in their own lives. Some had their eyes closed, most likely dreaming of a better life. Some read, flaunting their past lives at the clever table. Some just sat there; they looked the saddest, the most defeated, the most beaten by life. They looked like the ones who had given up. Without my airline ticket, I would have been one of them. Some were in small groups chattering, surrounded by suitcases. These were the happiest people, and even though I was not chatting, I did have a case. Today I belonged in that happy group, not the beaten-by-life group. I relaxed, and a smile may have even crept through me and escaped onto my face.

I'd never been to Heathrow before, but after riding the upward escalator from the tube line, I was instantly and suitably impressed at its size. I read the signs and headed for my terminal. I walked for miles and miles, gaining a quarter of an ounce of confidence with every step into the unknown.

There were hundreds of people, maybe thousands. Maths had never been one of my strong points, though I'm not sure what was my strong point – I was still searching for it and dreaming of it being a thing. There were far more people in this one airport than in my school, probably even more than the town I called home, all of them minding their own business. No one demanded anything of me, they all left me alone as I continued my long walk towards my check-in gate.

I wondered how I failed at being a child. Obviously I had not failed at actually being a child – I was once small and now I

Chapter 48

was bigger – but I had failed to enjoy childhood. Failed at the best years of my life. I never did childlike stuff. I was somehow always busy trying to keep myself safe. I was always guarded, trying to guess and prepare for what might be about to happen. I had been happiest in bed, and that thought saddened me. I did not think that was right. I did not think that being in bed daydreaming or sleeping should be a child's happiest memory. I had failed at being a child.

I reached my check-in counter. There was already a very long queue.

I was really only here in this queue because of Miss English. Sure, Mum had done all the preparation work, all the writing off for information and reading what information was returned. We planned it together, so I was here in this queue thanks to my mum as well, but Miss English had given me a future in a way my mum was unqualified and unable to do.

I was going to find friends, true friends – once I worked out what a true friend was. I would leave my old school friends where they were, unidentified on the yearly class photo. Today, I was leaving it all behind. It was in my past, completed, finished. It didn't matter that I had failed; that was history now. With every small shuffle towards the check-in counter, I moved further from my past tense.

I told myself that I did not have to go back to Grantown, but I knew I was lying. Someone would die or get married and I would have to return, but I pledged to myself that I would go back only as a visitor. I would go back to the holiday village as a holidayer. I would carry with me tales from some other faraway place that I would call home.

I checked in and swapped the first page of my book of ticket coupons for a boarding pass. I now had to clear customs and find my gate; more queues, more waiting, zero harassment. Just lots of time to think of whatever I wanted. I wasn't daydreaming, I wasn't wasting time, I was queuing. I was legitimately waiting, my mind free to think of what it liked. I was in fact multitasking, and there was nobody to tell me I was doing it wrong.

Ernest Hemingway escaped his home, with its broad lawns and narrow minds, when he was eighteen. He had to join the First World War to escape. He went halfway across the world from Oak Park to Paris; I was holding a boarding pass for a similar distance (though to a different destination) for possibly similar reasons at the same age. Unlike him, I was not joining a war – I was leaving one behind.

I was going to make the best of this adventure. I was going to turn things around. I was going to have a fresh start. I would leave my troubles behind and never mention them again. No one needed to know I was daft, then mental, then almost not stupid. All they needed to know was that I was Rhona, and if they did not like that then fine, I would not like them.

I found my gate. Boarding had not started, so I took a seat and waited for the doors to my new life to open.

I thought about my parents, about my family who had supported me, but was that support? Where had my parents gone wrong? Had they gone wrong, or had they done what was required and expected of parenting? I wasted hours practising words that would desert my brain the following day, then wasted more hours the following evening just to attain the same results. My parents had also wasted hours as well. I could have been out playing, learning the rules of friendships or finding a place where I fit in with my peers, my school, my hometown.

I think I appreciated the effort my mother made – not at the time, but now, sat here at my gateway to Australia. She, they, both cared enough to put in the extra hours. Sadly, I was still

Chapter 48

lost when I saw those homework words at the teacher's desk the following day. The extra hours appeared to be a pointless waste of everyone's time, at least to me. But were sayings like "practice makes perfect," "if at first you don't succeed, try, try again," or "you can do anything if you try hard enough" true? Granted, these sentences are encouraging, but are they not setting the kid up for failure? The stars will always be out of reach, no matter how far you stretch your arms up. If I were in my mother's position, I would choose honesty. I would be encouraging and realistic. Practice does not make perfect. Practice makes better, like with dancing and swimming. Rather than try, try, try again, failing at each step, I would stop, assess the situation, and find a way round the problem.

There are many ways to a destination, and we do not all have to choose the most direct route. Evan, who I tried so closely to follow – including waiting to get on a 747 to go to Australia, although I'm sure the idea was mine first – has a first-class honours degree in Pure Mathematics from Warwick University. He is now completing a postgraduate at Cambridge, and next year he will start his maths doctorate at Imperial College London. Pretty damn good for a boy who could not complete basic maths. His Primary Six teacher must be so proud that she spent so much time redoing those basic math steps with Evan.

There was movement around me. People were boarding; all I had to do was stand up and join them. And so I did.

I stood up and left my schooling behind, rooted in haunting memories. I was moving on. I was boarding.

I was no longer going to allow people to negatively affect me. I would be my own judge and jury. From now on, I would deal with facts. I would be honest, and I would expect honesty in return.

I would rely on no-one's opinions of me. If someone broke

my trust, I would simply cross him or her from necessity in my life and pop them onto my Do Not Trust list. There would be no return for them, no second chances. No one would come off the list.

I found my allotted window seat and slipped into position for the longest flight of my life. I then took a few deep, excited breaths. Many times I thought this moment was only a dream, a daft dream to go along with my stupid ideas, but not this time. This time, something good was actually happening to me. Today, my Phileas Fogg was real.

"Ladies and gentlemen, welcome on board British Airways flight number fifteen to Hong Kong, continuing onto Sydney."

"If the reader prefers, this book may be regarded as fiction. But there is always the chance that such a book of fiction may throw some light on what has been written as fact."
—**Ernest Hemingway,** *A Moveable Feast*

"Any man's life, told truly, is a novel..."
—**Ernest Hemingway,** *Death in the Afternoon*

Epilogue: The Best Years

The trip to Australia was everything I had hoped it would be. My Auntie Helen and Uncle Don in Sydney were exceedingly kind to me. Their home was my base as I spent eight months extensively travelling the continent. I had loved the freedom and ability to be anonymous while travelling around Australia as it had given me the ability to pretend I was anything I wanted to be. It had shown me there was a world outside of my sleepy hometown cemented in the Scottish Highlands. It was a world I could survive in, maybe even bloom in. As I was flying back to the UK after my first eight months of freedom, I knew I'd be departing and revamping myself again. My only reason for returning to the UK was to train for my chosen career as I knew an income was essential to support my next travelling venture, my next escape.

Since leaving secondary school, I have never accepted any charity which could have helped with my reading and spelling shortfalls. I carry the shame of being singled out as lazy, immature, or stupid in primary school very close to my heart, and so appearing normal remains paramount. While studying to be a nurse, my reading of textbooks was prolonged as they had to be read and re-read before I could fathom what the text was representing. It was not a fairytale story trapped within the covers of the book, it was anatomy and physiology that had to be understood before I could qualify, before I could travel again.

My assignments took longer to plan, prepare for, and write or type. I donated substantially more time to my studies than my peers. I willingly forewent an A+ on assignments and acknowledged comments like "A lot of careless spelling mistakes'" or "Spelling and grammar need attention throughout, but nevertheless this is a good sound piece of work" or "There are many typing errors which fortunately do not make your work incomprehensible but do distract, ensure proofreading always" as trade-offs for being considered normal.

After qualifying, it was time to move from Glasgow and leave my assignment markers behind. If they got together and discussed the common trends in my work, they may suggest that I was dyslexic.

I never chose cardiac nursing – I could not even spell coronary when I started. Instead, I chose Oxford. It was close to my now London-based brother, and no one I knew was in Oxford. I could have another fresh start. The only newly-graduated nursing job in Oxford was a rotation between cardiology and coronary care, and so it was the only job I applied for on qualifying. My father had died six months prior from a cardiac arrhythmia, so the small minds of the small town could make sense of my choice of speciality. I hoped that having exposure to two nursing areas would increase the possibility of me succeeding at one of them.

I found the language of cardiac nursing heavily abbreviated, which worked to my advantage. It did not matter that I could not spell myocardial infarction, I was usually writing MI. I couldn't spell cerebrovascular, but CVA did not cause me a

Epilogue: The Best Years

problem. A transient ischemic attack was a TIA. Ventricular fibrillation was VF. Abdominal aortic aneurysm was an AAA. I didn't even have to worry about it being peace in our time or a piece of cake, it was RIP. I learned the abbreviations for cardiac nursing and felt vulnerable when not surrounded by cardiac patients.

I liked the night shift. I liked that the people in the hospital were only the people that needed to be there. Nights were not full of overbearing relatives and their awkward questions. Seven nights on was followed by seven nights off, which to me meant five days being anonymous in Europe, usually in Italy.

I grew a little fatigued of Oxford so I moved to London, but I retreated back to the area when I didn't like my London job, its people, or the huge commute. I was still tired of Oxford but most of the staff and the work suited me. I had even made three friends. I bought what I needed and saved most of my money.

I travelled throughout New Zealand for six months before returning to Oxford to save again, and then I took off to the United States and Canada for four months. Then I got myself in a job in Sydney and tried hard to make Sydney my home. Something didn't fit, and six months later I tried to make Melbourne home. With every pack up and move I got a new chance to introduce myself to my new city and my new colleagues. I got to try again at being me.

As I looked for a place to live in Melbourne, I walked past a notice in a terraced window that said "Do you want to live here? $160 per week." The price was easily within my bracket and the location was perfect – twenty minutes' walk from the hospital at worst – so I figured there must be something wrong with it. However, after an unsuccessful showing at another place, I figured I might as well find out what the issue was.

I was greeted by a tall, lanky lad in an oversized orange jumper, complete with a blonde afro. He showed me around as I tried to discern if his plan was to murder me. I tried my best to work out what was wrong with the place, but I came up empty.

A week later, I moved in.

I would discover that the tall, lanky lad who oozed confidence was a Kiwi. He was brutally honest, always the centre of any party and the leader of any and all practical jokes. He hadn't been the cleverest kid in his year, and he hadn't always oozed confidence. He talked about being frightened of being beaten up by the local Maori and Samoan boys and girls. He skateboarded to escape his troubles and fears. He now throws up a massive two fingers to the peers that troubled him at school and does not give a shit about what they think of him. I laughed with him, at him even, giving him the encouragement to act even sillier. This was someone I could learn from.

A year later, we moved to London. Our goal was to save the valuable British pounds and move permanently to New Zealand. We found a flat in Vauxhall so I found a job in St Thomas, a twenty minute walking commute by the River Thames. Coming home after night shifts I often stopped in at the Tate and sat looking at Turner.

We got cheap flights to Europe and did lots of day trips out of London, but mainly we saved. We bought an engagement ring after he asked me in Paris to put up with his silly antics until he kicked the bucket.

Foreign languages had never been one of my strengths, but my Kiwi had previously lived in Venezuela and could speak Latin American Spanish. So, we travelled to Mexico. The Mexicans were overly helpful whenever we went into any shop. My prank-loving fiancée taught me how to say "I'm just looking

Epilogue: The Best Years

please," and I practiced my phrase *"omleta de queso"* and used it several times a day. This continued until while eating lunch with friends, one asked how I was getting on with "the attention." I replied my well-used phrase, to which she enquired, "Why are you asking for a cheese omelette?" Going by my previously-set rule around trust, I should have ditched my Kiwi there and then – instead, I laughed at him, and at my own gullibility. We swapped wedding rings a few days later.

In 2005, we exchanged our pounds for dollars and bought two one-way tickets to Auckland.

I worked in a Cardiac Cath lab for several years, during which time I got more and more involved in research. When doctors asked what the protocol stated, I would find the page and hold it in front of their scrubs, out from the sterile area. They would naturally read, unaware that I had just avoided reading aloud.

After seven years – my longest time in any job – I jumped ship, and after a few leaky boats I found a place in a privately-owned New Zealand pharmaceutical company. I still work with a bunch of tricks. When presenting, my slides are minimalistic, often just showing pictures, and my presentation comes from my head. I don't write notes in meetings, but instead use my memory until I get back to my office and my computer to make what notes I need.

I seldom return to Scotland, and when I do it is only as a holidayer. I met the Wobetide boy on a trip back to Scotland when he sold my mother some cheese. The wonder child, the child who could do everything and anything, sells cheese ten miles from where we went to school. He had everything and did nothing with his ability. Deep down I know he still can do everything and anything, but he has chosen not to for whatever reason.

I kept my promise to myself – I have no children. I have

not risked a child having to fight like I had to. However, my husband and I have rescued and rehomed several animals. I am a volunteer at the local animal rescue centre since 2009 and volunteered in an Elephant Sanctuary in South East Asia, although my time there was limited to within a holiday. I love traveling, it is no longer an opportunity to reinvent myself. I am happy with who I am. I travel to experience the world, not escape it. I try and use cruelty-free and sustainable friendly products. I cannot change the world and people's misuse of it, but I can choose not to be part of the problem or at least do a bit to help.

My bookshelf at home continues to expand. I am an avid reader of non-fiction and autobiography works and remain a Hemingway fan. I have visited Oak Park, Paris, Milan, and Key West, and in 2016 I fulfilled a long-standing dream of visiting East Africa. My books with their perfect spines hold my secrets. Some are read, some are abandoned, and some were bought with no intention of ever being read, but you wouldn't know by looking at them how many were in each category.

When I look up from the keyboard and see a sea of underlined red words, I try not to think of the red pen from school that used to drown my work and instead simply right click over each word in turn and try and pick the correct word from a list of words than my mind could easily exchange. I press send hoping that not too many words are wrong, and when someone replies with a sly comment about my trail rather than a trial I remind myself that this is the trade-off I have chosen in order to appear normal.

Even today, when an Ethics Committee is reviewing a trial protocol or an Investigators Brochure – both of which I've spent copious amounts of my personal hours working on – and comments about "their disappointment in the volume of

Epilogue: The Best Years

typographical errors," I try and not be disappointed. I simply thank them for their comment and start proofreading once again. I have come to the conclusion that people enjoy picking out faults in other people's work – it makes them feel better about themselves, which says more about them than about me. So long as the meaning is not lost, I'm content to live alongside a few typos.

I remain cautious of people, believing trust must be earned and if broken cannot be repaired. My list of foes continues. I do not consider myself clever, but I do consider myself smart.

I hear and see great modern-day dyslexics like Steven Spielberg, Richard Branson, and Jamie Oliver. Youtube is chocked-full of dyslexics being proud of their unique set of skills, their creativity, their ability to think out from a set of rules or regulations, out from the box. I somehow can't share their pride. I'm not a self-made millionaire. So what if forty percent self-made millionaires are dyslexics; sixty percent aren't. I see Steve Jobs unquestionable career success laced with luck rather than his dyslexia gift.

Like a library jammed full of books with only a fraction of them available on audiobooks and within my easy access, I live in a crammed and astonishing world, but only a fraction of it is easily available for me. I will always struggle; things will always take me infinitely longer than others to read, understand, and write down. However, I'm incredibly stubborn, and I will not admit defeat. Not only will I read books, but I'll write one. I'm not always going to get it right, but even when I'm knocked down and crippled with fatigue I'll drag myself vertical, dust off the latest hurt, and keep edging forwards. The alternative is to be trampled; the alternative is to let the primary teacher win and fail my secondary teacher along with myself.

There is no guidebook, textbook, or instructions on how to

adapt to dyslexia. It is a very individual and personal road, and sometimes it can be hard to see a way forwards. Other times, you may feel you are one hundred percent on the correct road, only to find you have travelled on the wrong road the whole time. Those "wrong roads" bring experiences that "normal" people don't get. Why blast up the highway when the b-roads are so much prettier?

If you find yourself on a journey not unlike my own, remember to keep moving, keep travelling, and keep adapting to the challenges. It is most certainly going to lead you on an insightful journey to a wonderful destination.

Acknowledgements

I have come across many teachers; most were, at their very best, terrible, and some were almost adequate. There was one, however, who worked tirelessly to undo the work done by all the others. My main thanks goes to my lifesaver, Mrs Jane McDowell, my English teacher who not only believed in me but saw a future for me long, long before I even allowed the possibility of succeeding or merely surviving to enter my own head. She knew me better than I knew myself. She understood how my broken brain operated and had solutions to enable it to work to its best capabilities.

The fact that my reader and scribe was Mrs Mitchell was no coincidence, but it took me until writing this book to realise it. I think of and silently thank Mrs McDowell daily. It utterly terrifies me to think of what or where I may have ended up if I had never sat in her English class. My endless gratitude is all I can offer in return.

Another thank you goes to my dear friend Miss Sarah Watt who, while we holidayed in New Caledonia, listened to a few of the stories that are captured within these pages. She was visibly moved by the debate of whether it was better to be mad and stupid, or to be just stupid. She gave me endless encouragement throughout the years of writing. She truly believed I held an important story within. She vowed to be my editor. By the time I got my story written she was Mrs Sarah Dillaman and had swapped her high-flying corporate role to pursue a career in teaching. She is now an English teacher as well as my first editor.

Thank you to the animals that have allowed me to be part of their lives, always happy to see me, always ready to forget the day's problems and have some fun. Never once was I not good enough for them. Never once did they take pleasure in my pain. Never once did they question, never once did they judge. All they ever asked for was my presence. With note to Hammy, my brother's hamster: I'm so very sorry, sadly you are the exception to some of the above statements. I maintain my plea of accidental hamster-slaughter as fact, but I admit defeat and my family's verdict of guilty remains on my scorecard of life.

Thanks to my brothers Calum and Evan who showed me two different train tracks that lead to different destinations in life, neither of which is more right or wrong than the other. By default, I also need to thank Frank Saunders, Mr Physics. Although I never sat in his class, he helped Evan clear his path of obstacles and showed him a brighter future. As I attempted to follow Evan down his track, my track was maybe more constructed because of Evan's crossing with Frank Saunders.

To my parents, William and Esther, I am sorry I was a problem child. I am sorry I never found the words to explain anything properly. Thirty-plus years later, looking back, I am sure you did your best, and that is the most anyone can expect.

Thanks also to my husband, David, who has been so supportive and encouraging in my everyday traumas. To my friends and my work colleagues, past and present, who either protected my

Acknowledgements

truths, are blissfully unaware of them, or simply do not care, thank you all for whichever you answered.

And to you, the reader, thank you for choosing me in the form of this book and sticking with me. I hope we all become more aware and more accepting of our differences, strengths, and limitations as a result.

Rhona Macdonald

Afterword

Rhona,

I have laughed, I have cried, and I have cried and laughed again all the way through your book. It sure took a lot of willpower, hard work, and many long hours for you to write it. Your memories are crystal clear in your mind and you read me very well in that I did not understand not only your problem but also your dark thoughts, as you didn't share them with me.

On parents' nights we were told that there was a stumbling block holding you back in reading but that you were working very hard. When we explained to Campbell (the headmaster and teacher from the World Map Day) how unhappy you were, he kept reassuring us that all the teachers were doing their best to help. The first person that explained the "stumbling block" as it was called was Eleanor Walker, your Primary Seven teacher. She was the one I recall telling me about dyslexia. I know it was not confirmed until Secondary One (Jane McDowell), as you say in the book, but did Eleanor Walker not get the ball rolling by getting a Record of Needs set up for you before leaving Primary?

I do recall travelling through to Inverness for a meeting after you were diagnosed. Judy Mitchell (your reader and scribe) attended that meeting and tried to help me by explaining how much help and assistance would be available and that the diagnosis was a good step forward. The events that happened after your diagnosis are what changed your ability and your belief in yourself. There is no denying the investigation should have commenced in Primary Two, but we did not have the access to the information that is freely available today.

Good luck with the publishing of your book, and may it give

Afterword

encouragement to others to follow their dreams, no matter the stumbling blocks they may face. You certainly fought a good fight and won. With much love, and very well done.

by: Rhona's mother, Esther Macdonald

Author Biography

Rhona Macdonald was born and raised in the remote Highlands of Scotland. She was 12 years old when she was tested and confirmed as being dyslexic, she has spent her life struggling, developing coping strategies and ultimately thriving due to her dyslexia. This is Rhona's first novel putting to use her exceptional memory as she recounts the years before and after her diagnosis. She is proud to prove to the teacher who bullied her that she is now a published author, despite her dyslexia. Rhona now lives in Auckland, New Zealand with her husband and their collection of rescued animals.

More About the Author

Email:
authorrhonamacdonald@gmail.com

Website:
www.escapingtheforest.com

Facebook:
www.facebook.com/Author-Rhona-Macdonald-342525873180160/

www.ingramcontent.com/pod-product-compliance
Lightning Source LLC
Chambersburg PA
CBHW051352290426
44108CB00015B/1984